Analogue Guide

Copenhagen

Contents

Copenhagen

–Welcome to Analogue Copenhagen

No small capital punches as much above its weight as Copenhagen. Off the radar for much of the 20th century and home to only a million plus people, the city has in the past decade or two firmly established itself among the global design, fashion and culinary avant-garde.

Copenhagen's place in the world is closely linked to its location at the crossroads of Scandinavia and the European mainland. The city first gained prominence in the 12th century as a fishing port and trading hub; hence its name København, or "merchants' harbour". The city experienced a major boost under the reign of Christian IV in the early 1600s, who turned Copenhagen from a successful town into a major capital. After a destitute but creative early 18th century Golden Age, Denmark entered a period of political neutrality and relative social stability. Inspired by central European modernism, yet free of its political associations, the post WWII years saw the first international wave of Danish modern design, including the likes of Finn Juhl and Arne Jacobsen.

Since the 1990s, Copenhagen has undergone another transformation: from a small Scandinavian capital to an open, international, bijou-size metropolis. A major contributing factor was the opening of the Øresund Bridge in 2000, which directly linked Copenhagen to the south of Sweden. A host of talent from Denmark and across the globe has picked up on the city's penchant for design, while its relaxed culture is complemented by a serious culinary dimension. We have set out to assemble the best of all of this, from independent design outlets to urban beaches and foodie highlights in formerly neglected inner-city neighbourhoods. Enjoy!

Neighbourhoods

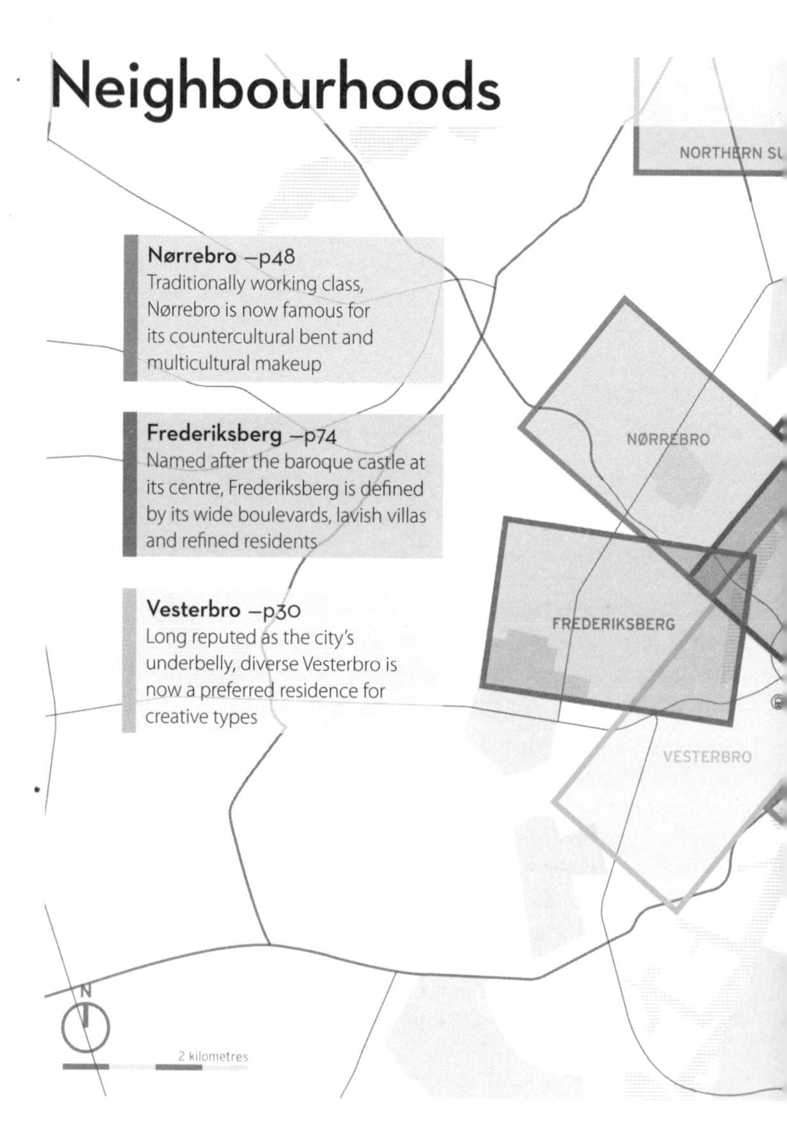

Nørrebro –p48
Traditionally working class, Nørrebro is now famous for its countercultural bent and multicultural makeup

Frederiksberg –p74
Named after the baroque castle at its centre, Frederiksberg is defined by its wide boulevards, lavish villas and refined residents

Vesterbro –p30
Long reputed as the city's underbelly, diverse Vesterbro is now a preferred residence for creative types

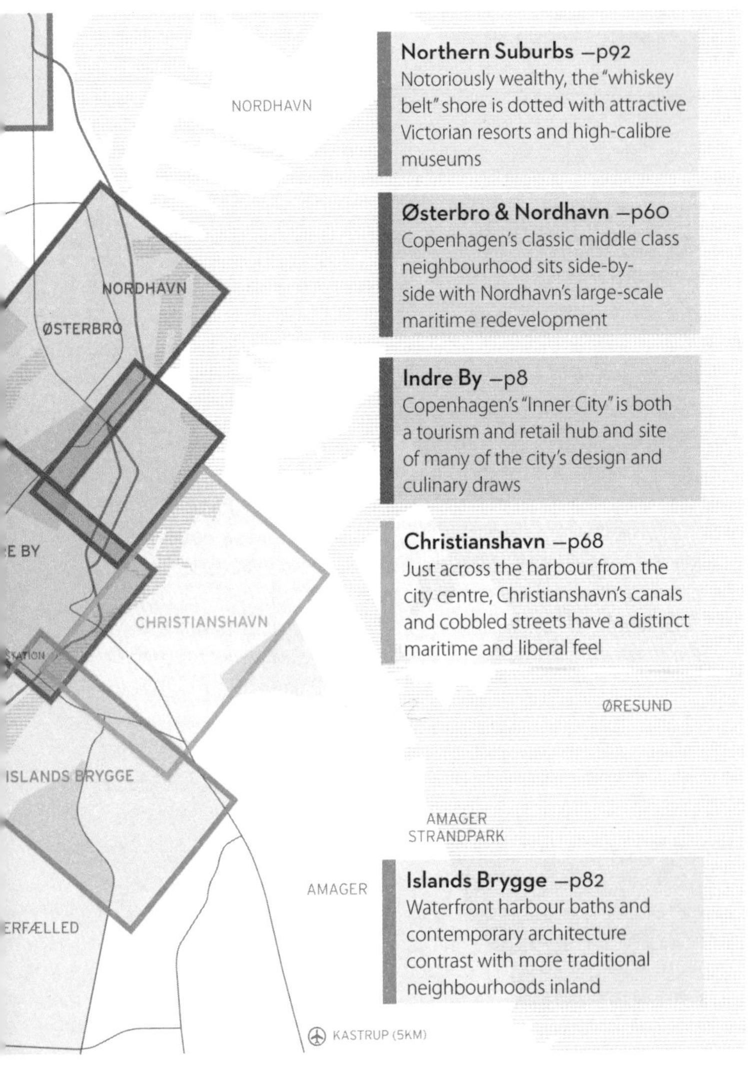

Northern Suburbs –p92
Notoriously wealthy, the "whiskey belt" shore is dotted with attractive Victorian resorts and high-calibre museums

Østerbro & Nordhavn –p60
Copenhagen's classic middle class neighbourhood sits side-by-side with Nordhavn's large-scale maritime redevelopment

Indre By –p8
Copenhagen's "Inner City" is both a tourism and retail hub and site of many of the city's design and culinary draws

Christianshavn –p68
Just across the harbour from the city centre, Christianshavn's canals and cobbled streets have a distinct maritime and liberal feel

Islands Brygge –p82
Waterfront harbour baths and contemporary architecture contrast with more traditional neighbourhoods inland

Indre By

–Copenhagen's Social and Political Centre

Indre By, literally Copenhagen's "Inner City", is the historical, geographical and political centre of the capital. Densely built up with medieval architecture, church spires and narrow streets, it is also the city's retail and tourism hub, as well as the site of the royal palace and the postcard-pretty Nyhavn museum harbour.

Copenhagen dates back to the 12th century when the Bishop of Roskilde built the city's first castle on Slotsholmen island—today the site of the vast neo-baroque Christiansborg Palace, which houses all branches of government. In the 17th century, the medieval city experienced large-scale transformations during the reign of King Christian IV, who ventured to make Copenhagen his grand capital. Inspired by the wealth of Amsterdam and the *grandeur* of Louis XIV, his projects included vast fortifications, the new settlements of Nyboder and Christianshavn (p68), Rosenborg Castle, and the baroque Frederiksberg Palace (see p74) summer residence. The medieval old town contrasts with the adjacent 18th century *Frederiksstaden*, with its Cartesian layout, broad streets, stately mansions and, at its centre, Amalienborg Palace, the royal residence. Finally permitted to outgrow its fortifications in 1853, Copenhagen saw a flurry of development, including the building of its Central Station, Denmark's National Gallery, the tranquil Botanical Gardens and the classic Tivoli amusement park.

Though Copenhagen's centre hosts more than its fair share of brash tourist attractions, fast food outlets and mid-range retail, it is also the site of many of the city's main draws, including a plethora of famous design outlets and culinary highlights. As a rule of thumb, more refined options can generally be found away from the bustle of Tivoli and closer to *Kongens Have* park.

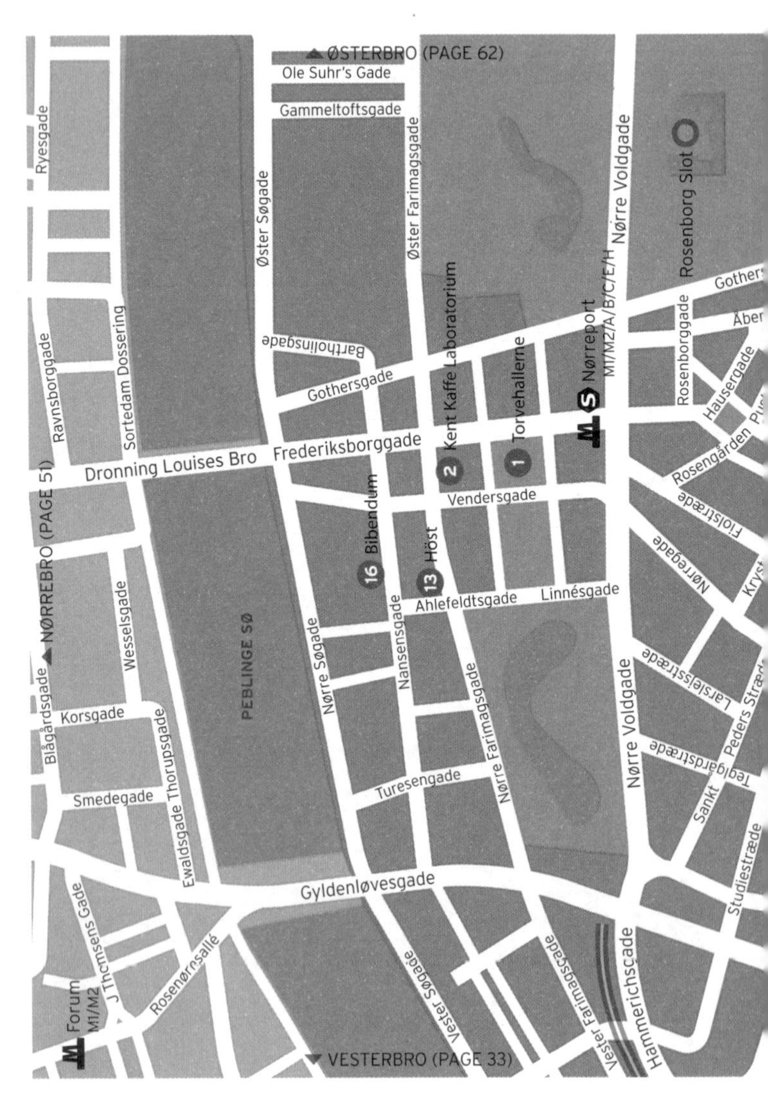

ØSTERBRO (PAGE 62)
Ole Suhr's Gade
Gammeltoftsgade
Ryesgade
Øster Søgade
Øster Farimagsgade
Nørre Voldgade
Rosenborg Slot
Kent Kaffe Laboratorium
Torvehallerne
Nørreport
M1/M2/A/B/C/E/H
Barthollinsgade
Gothersgade
Ravnsborggade
Sortedam Dossering
Frederiksborggade
Dronning Louises Bro
Rosenborggade
Hausergade
Rosengården
Vendersgade
Fiolstræde
Nørregade
NØRREBRO (PAGE 51)
Bibendum
Höst
Ahlefeldtsgade
Linnésgade
Wesselsgade
PEBLINGE SØ
Nørre Søgade
Nansensgade
Nørre Farimagsgade
Larslejsstræde
Pedersstræde
Blågårdsgade
Korsgade
Ewaldsgade
Thorupsgade
Teglgårdstræde
Nørre Voldgade
Turesengade
Smedegade
Sankt
Studiestræde
Gyldenløvesgade
J Thomsens Gade
Rosenørnsallé
Vester Søgade
Vester Farimagsgade
Hammerichsgade
Forum
M1/M2
VESTERBRO (PAGE 33)

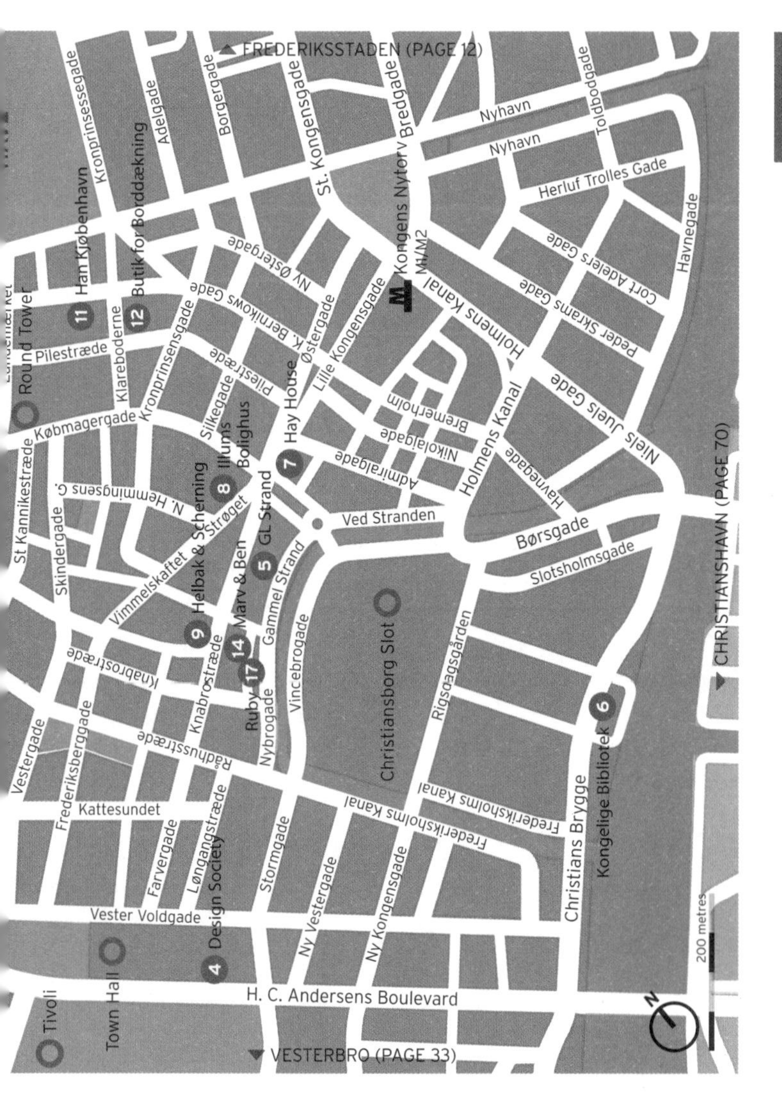
FREDERIKSSTADEN (PAGE 12)
VESTERBRO (PAGE 33)
CHRISTIANSHAVN (PAGE 70)
Kronprinsessegade
Adelgade
Borgergade
St. Kongensgade
Bredgade
Nyhavn
Nyhavn
Toldbodgade
Herluf Trolles Gade
Havnegade
Cort Adelers Gade
Peder Skrams Gade
Niels Juels Gade
Holmens Kanal
Holmens Kanal
Kongens Nytorv
M1/M2
Ny Østergade
K. Bernikows Gade
Østergade
Lille Kongensgade
Bremerholm
Nikolajgade
Admiralgade
Havnegade
Ved Stranden
Børsgade
Slotsholmsgade
Christiansborg Slot
Rigsdagsgården
Vincebrogade
Gammel Strand
Nybrogade
Frederiksholms Kanal
Frederiksholms Kanal
Christians Brygge
Kongelige Bibliotek
6
Ny Kongensgade
Ny Vestergade
Stormgade
H. C. Andersens Boulevard
Vester Voldgade
Løngangstræde
Farvergade
Kattesundet
Frederiksberggade
Vestergade
Rådhusstræde
Knabrostræde
Knabrostræde
Skindergade
St Kannikestræde
N. Hemmingsens G.
Vimmelskaftet
Strøget
Købmagergade
Kronprinsensgade
Klareboderne
Pilestræde
Pilestræde
Silkegade
11 Han Kjøbenhavn
12 Butik for Borddækning
Round Tower
7 Hay House
8 Illums Bolighus
9 Helbak & Scherning
5 GL Strand
14 Marv & Ben
17 Ruby
4 Design Society
Town Hall
Tivoli
200 metres
N

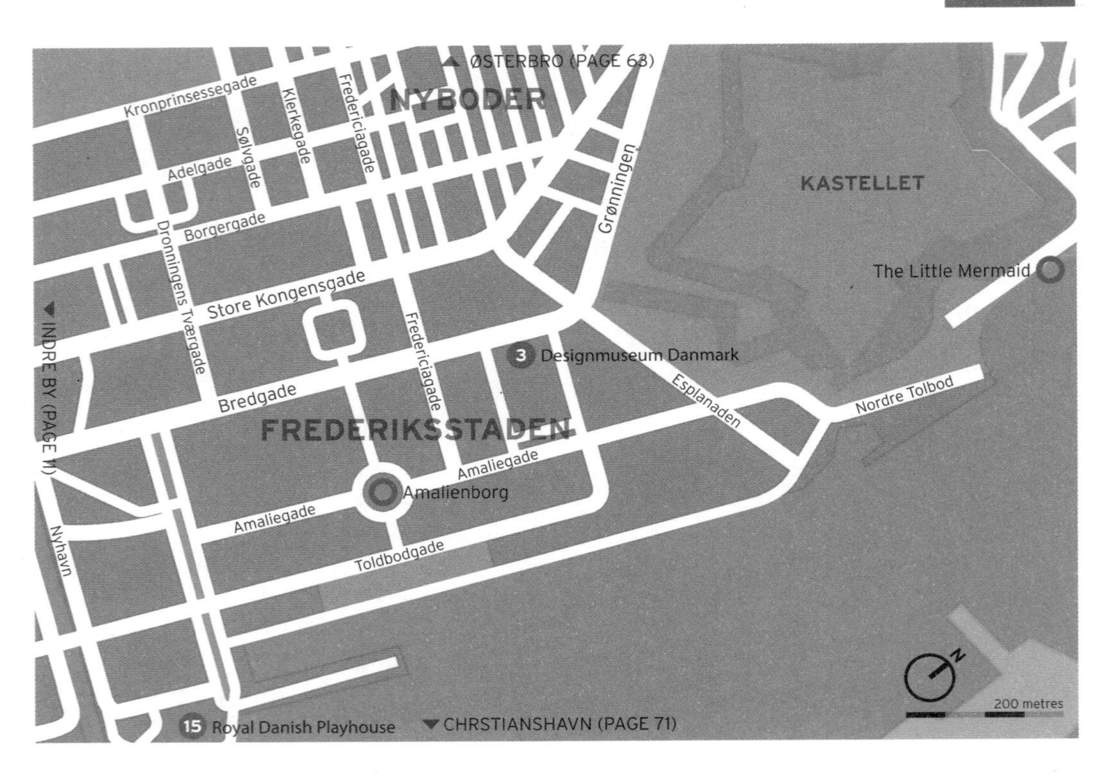
ØSTERBRO (PAGE 63)
NYBODER
Kronprinsessegade
Klerkegade
Fredericiagade
Sølvgade
Adelgade
Borgergade
Grønningen
KASTELLET
The Little Mermaid
Dronningens Tværgade
Store Kongensgade
Fredericiagade
3 Designmuseum Danmark
INDRE BY (PAGE 11)
Bredgade
Esplanaden
Nordre Tolbod
FREDERIKSSTADEN
Amaliegade
Amalienborg
Amaliegade
Toldbodgade
Nyhavn
N
200 metres
15 Royal Danish Playhouse
CHRSTIANSHAVN (PAGE 71)

Upscale Market

Torvehallerne

1 Frederiksborggade 21
+45 70 10 60 70
torvehallernekbh.dk
Nørreport M1 M2 S
Open daily. Mon-Thu 10am-7pm; Fri 10am-8pm; Sat 10am-6pm; Sun 11am-5pm
Café and bakery Mon-Fri from 7am; Sat/Sun from 8am

Opened as recently as 2011, this upscale covered market is already a city institution and evidence of how far Copenhagen has come as a serious culinary destination. Israels Plads was the site of the city's original vegetable market, but when it was moved to the suburbs in 1958, the square fell into neglect as a car park. Today, the 60 stands in the market's two halls cover everything from fresh fish and organic sausage to sushi and a cava bar.

Coffee Lab

Kent Kaffe Laboratorium

2 Nørre Farimagsgade 70
+45 33 11 13 15
kentkaffelaboratorium.com
Nørreport M1 M2 S
Open daily. Mon-Fri 9am-5.30pm; Sat 11am-5pm; Sun noon-5pm

As its name suggests, Kent melds the arts and sciences of the bean at its Nørreport laboratory. This being Denmark, science is firmly underscored by good design, and attractive mid-century furniture dots the café's living room area. With a small in-house roaster and five different brewing methods, this is the place to come for an experimental, but unfailingly delicious organic jolt. The mission of Kent's barristas is to re-familiarise its clientele with the subtle nuances and unchartered potential of coffee drunk black and filtered. Pair your Chemex brew with a fresh *smørrebrød*.

From Rococo to Danish Modern

Designmuseum Danmark

3 Bredgade 68
+45 33 18 56 50
designmuseum.dk
Østerport S, Kongens Nytorv M1 M2
Closed Mon. Open Tue-Sun 11am-5pm; Wed until 9pm
Admission DKK 75 (€10)

Housed in the former Royal Fredrik's Hospital, a sumptuous example of Rococo architecture, the Designmuseum Danmark is one of Scandinavia's premier design museums and a forum for Danish and international design, industrial design, arts and crafts. Founded in 1890, the museum's very Danish remit has consistently been to promote a concept of quality in design. The museum's inspiring collection and exhibitions are heightened by a visit to the herringbone floored Café Klint whose glimmering rows of *smørrebrød* can also be enjoyed outside in the picturesque garden.

Where Designers Meet

Design Society

4 H. C. Andersens Boulevard 27
+45 33 69 33 69
designsociety.dk
København H S
Café open Mon-Fri 9am-5pm

With a mandate to promote innovative design solutions to common problems faced by society and the individual, the Design Society is a forum for the city's entrepreneurs, creatives, scientists and designers, offering workshops and lectures throughout the year. For the visitor to Copenhagen, the predictably well-designed café, with its gorgeous furniture, luxurious espresso and excellent Scandinavian snacks, is not to be missed. A collection of advanced materials is also open to the public.

Munch to Lynch

GL Strand

5 Gammel Strand 48
+45 33 36 02 60
glstrand.dk
Kongens Nytorv M1 M2
Closed Mon. Open Tue-Sun 11am-5pm; Wed 11am-8pm
Admission DKK 65 (€8.70)

Artist and professor C.W. Eckersberg founded GL Strand Arts Society in 1825 with the aim of bridging the gap between the elitist Art Academy and a public audience. Exhibiting such innovative artists as Edvard Munch in 1908, Asger Jorn in 1953 and more recently David Lynch and Henrik Vibskov (p22), the gallery has always been a staunch supporter of artists who dare to challenge tradition. Since 1952, the Society has been housed in a handsome Rococo mansion designed by acclaimed 18th century Dutch-Danish architect Philip de Lange.

Royal Diamond

Kongelige Bibliotek

6 Søren Kierkegaards Plads 1
+45 33 47 47 47
kb.dk
Kongens Nytorv M1 M2
Closed Sun. Open Mon-Sat 8am-10pm (July/August until 7pm)

Containing nearly all printed matter published in Danish since the inception of print in Denmark in 1482, the Nordic countries' most comprehensive library is a treasure trove of historical documentation. The library's main branch at Slotsholmen is split between the original early 20th century building and waterside Black Diamond, a glittery 1999 black marble and glass structure. The Black Diamond also houses a concert hall, shop and café with a generous, deck-chair-studded terrace overlooking Christianshavn (p68) across the harbour—one of the city's top summer spots.

Contemporary Danish Design

Hay House

7 Østergade 61
+45 99 42 44 00
hay.dk
Kongens Nytorv M1 M2,
Nørreport M1 M2 S
Closed Sun. Open Mon-Fri 10am-8pm; Sat 10am-5pm

Contemporary Danish designers the likes of Hay aim to lift Danish design out of the mid-20th century and into an exuberant, more internationally orientated future. Hay embodies this spirit to perfection, designing cutting edge furniture, gorgeous textiles and home wears to the delight of the design-savvy shopper. Check out the Hay House HQ, overlooking the streets of bustling Indre By, and discover the manifold delights conceived by the young Danish designers of today.

Design Emporium

Illums Bolighus

8 Amagertorv 10
+45 33 14 19 41
illumsbolighus.dk
Kongens Nytorv M1 M2,
Nørreport M1 M2 S
Open daily. Mon-Fri 10am-7pm; Sat 10am-6pm; Sun 11am-5pm

Founded in 1925 by Kaj Dessau, an entrepreneur with a keen aesthetic sense, Illums Bolighus (then known as BO) was conceived as a space where furnished interiors would freely interact with textiles and art. Dessau and his artistic director Brita Drewsen's avant-garde concept proved remarkably successful, helping to catapult Danish design to the forefront of the global scene. In its present incarnation, the elegant repository of the best of Danish design sits elegantly in architect Kay Korbing's multi-story 1960s edifice on Amargetorv.

Jewelry Meets Design

Helbak & Scherning

9 Kompagnistræde 8
+45 20 61 04 77
helbak-scherning.dk
Kongens Nytorv M1 M2,
Nørreport M1 M2 S
Closed Sun. Open Mon-Thu 11am-5.30pm; Fri 11am-6pm; Sat 11am-4pm

Occupying the lower and upper ground levels of a typical Indre By townhouse, Malene Helbak's versatile, brilliantly coloured collection of ceramics and Mette Scherning's contemporary jewelry make an ideal pair. Helbak's own line is complemented by pieces by a range of Danish homewear designers—think throws by RosenbergCPH alongside classics the likes of Finn Juhl's (p98) iconic tray. Whether it's a bracelet or a vase you're after, this is the place to find it.

New Nordic

Henrik Vibskov

10 Krystalgade 6
+45 33 14 61 00
henrikvibskovboutique.com
Nørreport M1 M2 S
Closed Sat/Sun. Open Mon-Thu 11am-6pm; Fri 11am-7pm

Maverick fashion designer Henrik Vibskov's Copenhagen boutique provides an excellent introduction to the wilds of the "New Nordic Movement". Here, Scandinavian minimalism is eschewed in favour of mutliculturally inspired eclecticism, underscored by uncompromising craftsmanship. Look out for items from Vibskov's "Piggy" series, featuring row upon row of pac-man like porcine countenances.

Kjøbenhavn's Aesthetes

Han Kjøbenhavn

11 Vognmagergade 7
+45 52 15 35 07
hankjobenhavn.com
Nørreport M1 M2 S
Closed Sun. Open Mon-Thu 11am-6pm; Fri 11am-7pm; Sat 10am-5pm

Its gorgeous aquamarine and honeycomb coloured interior decor would be reason enough to pay a visit, but this ultra-urban purveyor of menswear focussed on Danish clean lines, combined with the spirit of the "rowdy worker", is just as irresistible. Inspired by mid-century furniture design, jackets, eyewear and jeans are chiseled into contemporary classics worthy of the streets of København. Show yours off while hitting the bars of Vesterbro's meatpacking district (p30).

The Art of Tableware

Butik for Borddækning

12 Møntergade 6
+45 33 32 61 01
butikforborddaekning.dk
Nørreport M1 M2 S
Closed Sun. Open Mon-Fri 11am-6pm; Sat 11am-4pm

As much a gallery as a retail outlet, the "Shop for Table Settings" displays six designer/craftsmen's work reflecting different expressions of the art of tableware. Using materials such as glass, porcelain, earthenware, concrete and wood, each piece is designed with the intersection of gastronomy, good conversation and visual pleasure in mind. With styles ranging from traditional to radically innovative, the versatility of the Butik's collection is sure to complement the most divergent of tabletops. Exhibitions are also regularly held.

Best Designed New Nordic

Höst

13 Nørre Farimagsgade 41
+45 70 70 15 88
cofoco.dk/hoest
Nørreport M1 M2 S
Open daily 5.30pm-midnight

In 2012, Copenhagen restaurant group Cofoco joined forces with Menu and Norm Architects to produce Höst, an attractive bastion of New Nordic cuisine. The traditional-meets-contemporary seasonal menu incorporates Northern champions the likes of Norwegian lobster with seabuckthorn and juniper, blueberries with bog myrtle schnapps and a requisite smattering of truffles—to be enjoyed against the romance of an utterly urban-rustic backdrop.

Scandinavian Dining and Oenology

Marv & Ben

14 Snaregade 4
+45 33 91 01 91
marvogben.dk
Kongens Nytorv M1 M2
Closed Sun. Open Mon-Sat 6pm-10pm

Danish chef Fred Hvidt and Swedish sommelier Fredrik Nilsson's new Nordic restaurant is a fabulously understated yet wildly adventurous foray into the thick of new Nordic cuisine. Using only ingredients sourced within close range of Copenhagen, Hvid pickles, dries and sautées a wide range of Danish delicacies, from eller's pig's trotters to leeks found in the restaurant's own biodynamic garden. Nilsson's excellent selection of biodynamic and organic wines are a delight in of themselves.

Waterfront Theatre

Royal Danish Playhouse

15 Sankt Annæ Plads 36
+45 33 69 69 69

kglteater.dk

Kongens Nytorv M1 M2

Regular performances. Refer to website for program

With an illustrious history dating back to 1748, the Royal Danish Theatre once housed Denmark's premier dramatic, opera, ballet and concert halls and their respective academies under one roof at Kongens Nytorv. Today, the 1874 "Old Stage" and controversial 2005 Henning Larsen designed Opera House are joined by the centrally located Royal Danish Playhouse, a 2008 RIBA award-winning creation by architects Boje Lundgaard and Lene Tranberg, complete with stunning waterfront views. For fans of Dogme 95 and Danish television series, this is the place to catch the stars live.

European & New World Bottles

Bibendum

16 Nansensgade 45
+45 33 33 07 74
bibendum.dk
Nørreport M1 M2 S
Closed Sun. Open Mon-Sat 4pm-midnight

Cosy wine and small plates bar Bibendum assembles an inventive list of European bottles, jazzed up by some intriguing New World labels. Select from a delectable assortment of locally inspired dishes, such as herring with spring cheese and onion compote or langoustine with lemon and dill, ideally paired with a crisp glass of Grüner Veltliner from Austria's Kremstal region or a grassy Marlborough Sauvignon Blanc. The cellar-inspired interior and eclectic mix of patrons add to the fizz.

Cocktail Sophisticate

Ruby

Nybrogade 10
+45 33 93 12 03
rby.dk
Kongens Nytorv M1 M2
Open daily. Mon-Sat 4pm-2am; Sun 7pm-1am

Plush cocktail lounge Ruby is a central Copenhagen classic. Artful mixology blends perfectly with softly lit leather and marble clad interiors to create a sophisticated ambiance as well suited to a romantic evening as to a potent session of power drinking. Ever at the cutting edge of mixology, Ruby's latest concoctions include the Oloroso Martini, which adds a splash of Oloroso Sherry to the Gin, and Cynar Spritz, a racy retake on the classic spritz, combining Italian Cynar with Danish dill Aquavit, Elderflower syrup and a swig of dry champagne.

Vesterbro

–Gateway to the City

Located just outside Copenhagen's centre and main station area, Vesterbro has long maintained a reputation as the city's underbelly. The neighbourhood was associated with poverty, prostitution and drug trafficking for much of its history. Today, its central location, quaint architecture and diverse make-up make it a preferred residence for creative types and young professionals.

Vesterbro roughly translates as "the paved road leading into the city from the west", and for much of its history it was just that—it was prohibited, for military reasons, to settle outside the city limits. When modern warfare made the fortifications obsolete in the 19th century, the authorities finally allowed the development of Copenhagen's suburbs. Vesterbro's location by the water and on the main roads and railways connecting the capital to the rest of the country, made it attractive for industrial development, including the large Kødbyen (literally "Meat City") meatpacking district. As an impoverished neighbourhood in flux, Vesterbro soon became the city's red-light district. This status was accentuated after 1967 when Denmark was the first country in the world to formally legalise pornography. The neighbourhood maintained its legacy as the gateway to Copenhagen when, from the mid-20th century, its cheap rents attracted immigrants from all over the world.

A favourable place to live today, much of the neighbourhood is now made up of an alluring jumble of small boutiques, Pakistani grocers, quality coffee outlets and an eclectic mix of restaurants. Despite its overall gritty feel, only few of the red lights and associated crime remain, mostly near the Central Station. The Kødbyen meat market now houses galleries, hip restaurants, and advertising agencies and is a main focus of Copenhagen's nightlife.

GRANOLA

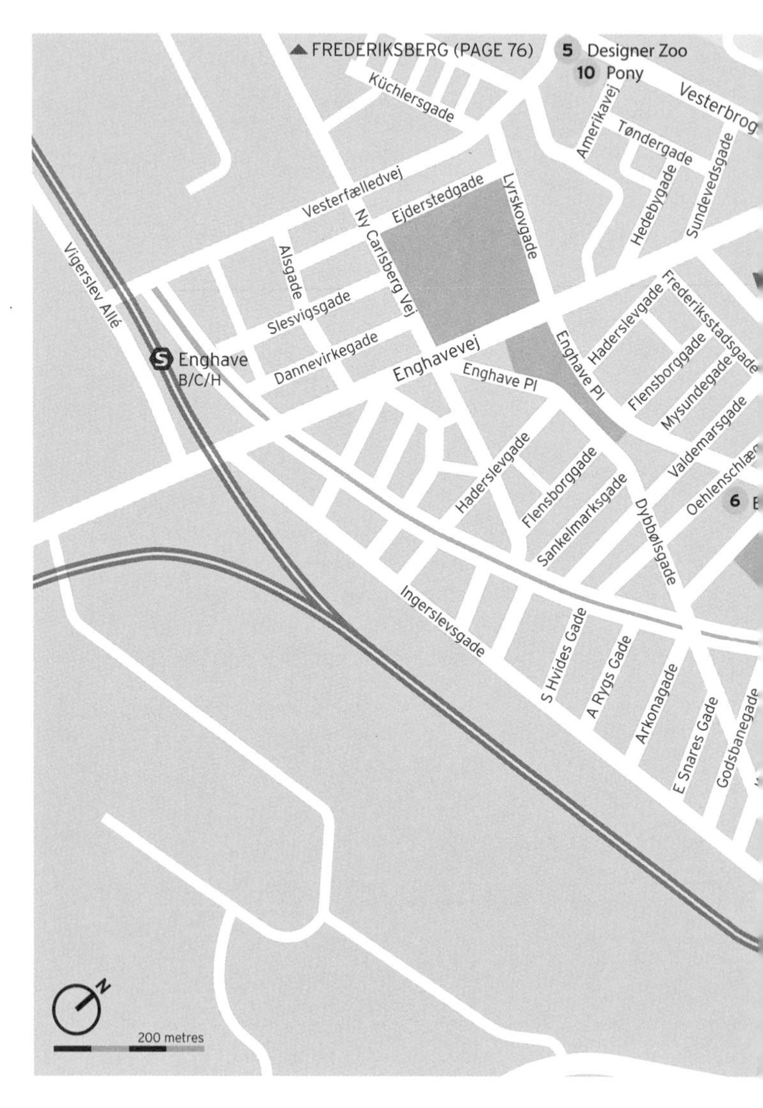
FREDERIKSBERG (PAGE 76)
5 Designer Zoo
10 Pony
Küchlersgade
Vesterbrog
Amerikavej
Tøndergade
Sundevedsgade
Hedebygade
Vesterfælledvej
Ejderstedgade
Lyrskovgade
Ny Carlsberg Vej
Alsgade
Slesvigsgade
Dannevirkegade
Vigerslev Allé
Enghave
B/C/H
Enghavevej
Enghave Pl
Enghave Pl
Haderslevgade
Frederiksstadsgade
Flensborggade
Mysundegade
Valdemarsgade
Oehlenschlæ
6
Haderslevgade
Flensborggade
Sankelmarksgade
Dybbølsgade
Ingerslevsgade
S Hvides Gade
A Rygs Gade
Arkonagade
E Snares Gade
Godsbanegade
200 metres

FREDERIKSBERG (PAGE 77)
Boyesgade
Guldsmeden
Frederiksberg Allé
Gl Kongevej
Forhåbningsholms Allé
Svanholmsvej
Schønbergsg.
Vodroffs Tværgade
N Ebbesens Vej
Vodroffsvej
Værnedamsvej
1 Central Hotel
13 Lidkoeb
P. Maries Allé
TERBRO
Kampmannsgade
SANKT JØRGENS SØ
Westend
Dannebrogsgade
Bagerstræde
Gammel Kongevej
Vester Søgade
Herholdtsgade
Nyropsgade
Es-Es
Vesterport
A/B/C/E/H
INDRE BY (PAGE 10)
3 Sort Kaffe & Vinyl
Skydebaneg.
Absalonsgade
Eskildsgade
Istedgade
Gasværksvej
Viktoriagade
Abel Cathrines Gade
11 Restaurant Cofoco
Vesterbrogade
Colbjørnsensgade
Reventlowsgade
Mother 8
9 Paté Paté
København H
A/B/C/E/H
København H
(Central Station)
7 Kødbyens Fiskebar
12 Karriere
Tivoli
Bernstorffsgade
KØDBYEN
Ingerslevsgade
Tietgensgade
Dybbølsbro
A/B/C/E/H
Stoltenbergsgade
O. Mønsteds Gade
ISLANDS BRYGGE (PAGE 84)

Urban Getaway

Central Hotel

1 Tullinsgade 1
+45 33 21 00 95
centralhotelogcafe.dk
København H Ⓢ
Doubles from DKK 1,800 (€240)/ night incl. tax

The Central Hotel offers elegant lodgings in a single cosy room. Located half a block from its sister establishment, local brunch favourite Granola (p79), the hotel is designed for couples planning a stylish Copenhagen getaway. Tastefully designed and meticulously appointed with Royal Eden and Geismar linen, the hotel is also remarkably convenient given its location between edgy Vesterbro and bourgeois Friedriksberg, not to mention its proximity to the centre of the city. Guests can enjoy breakfast in bed or pop over to Granola.

Sustainable Sleeps

Hotel Guldsmeden Bertrams

2 Vesterbrogade 107
+45 70 20 81 07
hotelguldsmeden.com
Enghave Ⓢ
Doubles from DKK 1,526 (€204)/ night incl. tax

Started by Sandra and Mark Weinert in Aarhus, the Guldsmeden Hotels have come to stand for a playful take on excellence in hospitality, melded with sustainability. In keeping with the hotel's ecological tendencies, Bertrams also has an excellent café serving sprightly organic snacks overlooking the lush greenery of the outdoor patio. The hotel's plush guest rooms are decorated with natural finishings and include beautiful pieces of art from several of the world's most far-flung climes.

Espresso Bites

Sort Kaffe & Vinyl

Skydebanegade 4
+45 61 70 33 49

Dybbølsbro Ⓢ

Open daily. Mon-Fri 8am-7pm; Sat/Sun 9am-7pm

Serving explosive brew from local pioneering roasters Risteriet, Sort Kaffe & Vinyl is also the place for the LP aficionado to stock up on scores of records. With an underground-cool vibe, the tiny café is a local favourite during the morning coffee rush and morphs into a relaxing spot to flick through the pages of a magazine as the day progresses. On a warm summer's day, enjoy your cup while lounging on the comfy chairs lining the front of the shop.

Curated Fashion

Es-Es

Istedgade 108
+45 33 22 48 28
es-es.dk
Dybbølsbro
Closed Sun. Open Mon-Fri 11am-6pm; Sat 11am-4pm

Tina Stampe's Istedgade boutique started out as a children's clothing store, but soon transformed itself into a repository of Danish and international women's fashion, beauty and accessories. Stampe's brilliantly curated selection includes knockout strappy sandals by Repetto, the latest Scandinavian trends by Bruuns Baazaar and Oskia London's luxurious range of facial and body care products.

Design in Action

Designer Zoo

5 Vesterbrogade 137
+45 33 24 94 93

dzoo.dk

Enghave 

Closed Sun. Open Mon-Thu 10am-5.30pm; Fri 10am-7pm; Sat 10am-3pm

On the western end of Vesterbrogade, Designer Zoo covers two spacious floors with the best in contemporary Danish design and craft. Exhibits change regularly and are complimented by seven active in-house workshops. Staffed by artists and designers, Designer Zoo is literally a storehouse of visual and intellectual information for the lover of great design.

Convivial Vini

Bevi Bevi

6 Oehlenschlægersgade 53
+45 31 67 21 20
Dybbølsbro S
Closed Sun-Wed. Open Thu-Sat
4pm-midnight

Delightful *vini e crostini* are served at this casual-chic wine bar. Owner Philip Skovgaard maintains a jovial ambiance and a top-flight selection of hand picked Italian bottles, accompanied by classics such as wild boar ragout and cheese polenta. Soak in the local scene as you jostle for space with a mix of artistic locals and bubbly visitors.

Eclectic Fish

Kødbyens Fiskebar

Flæsketorvet 100
+45 32 15 56 56
fiskebaren.dk
Dybbølsbro
Closed Sun/Mon. Open Tue-Thu 5.30pm-midnight; Fri/Sat 5.30pm-2am

In the heart of Vesterbro's former abbatoir-turned-hipster hangout Flaesketorvet, Kødbyens Fiskebar shells, grills and sautés the freshest selection of sustainably sourced fish. The restaurant's electric ambiance is heightened by its slick industrial décor and creatively inclined customers. Pop in for a handful of hand dived Norwegian clams or Lundfjorden blue mussels with a crisp glass of Riesling "boblar" from the Mosel.

Italian Soul Food

Mother

 Høkerboderne 9
+45 22 27 58 98
mother.dk
Dybbølsbro
Open daily 11am-11pm (Sun until 10pm)

A relative newcomer to the ever-trendy Kødbyen scene, Mother and her wood fire oven provide a scrumptious stream of Italian "soul food" to hungry Copenhageners. Delicious Neapolitan-style organic sourdough pizza, grilled meats and vegetables predominate, along with the restaurant's "micro-range" of Italian wines, imported directly from producers who the owners know personally. On warmer days the bustling space spills out onto outdoor communal seating, ideally suited to those long Scandinavian summer days.

Paté & Champagne

Paté Paté

Slagterboderne 1
+45 39 69 55 57

patepate.dk

Dybbølsbro Ⓢ

Closed Sun. Open Mon-Wed 9am-midnight; Thu 9am-1am; Fri 9am-3am; Sat 11am-3pm

Paté Paté is oenologically attuned brothers Kenn and Dan Husted's fabulous Vesterbro wine bar. Located in a former liver paté factory, Paté stays true to its carnivorous roots, spinning virtuoso renditions of tender Grilled Lamb Fillet on the rack and small plates, such as a creamy *paté de campagne* and wriggling fresh Irish oysters. Vegetarian options include Risotto with kale, Hokkaido pumpkin and spring onion. Pair these with the Husted's unbeatable 20-page wine list and you're set for a foodie's night on the town.

Compact but Powerful

Pony

10 Vesterbrogade 135
+45 33 22 10 00
ponykbh.dk
Enghave S
Closed Mon. Open Tue-Sun from 5.30pm

Galloping to the forefront of Copenhagen's cutting-edge foodie scene, Pony occupies culinary stalwart Kadeau's (p73) original Copenhagen spot and offers simple and natural renditions of creative dishes. Choose from the daily four-course menu, the "Pony Kick", or a selection of à la carte New Nordic options sourced locally, from Bornholm island and the restaurant's extensive "Scandinavian backyard". The wine list features a handful of carefully sourced European bottles from small, terroir driven producers. The atmosphere is welcoming and relaxed.

Nordic Bistro

Restaurant Cofoco

Abel Cathrines Gade 7
+45 33 13 60 60
cofoco.dk/cofoco
København H
Closed Sun. Open Mon-Sat 5.30pm-midnight

Copenhagen's local Cofoco group's first restaurant melds good design and an upbeat, urbane environment with excellent "Nordic bistro" fare. Spiritually positioning itself midway between the Northern Lights and Naples, Cofoco embodies Copenhagen's unique situation at the crossroads of the Nordic countries and the rest of Europe. Using locally sourced ingredients to create innovative versions of French and Southern European classics, rimmede scallops and pickled gooseberries will pop up in a mussel soup, just as *ramsløgsolie* (wild garlic oil) will accompany a grilled chicken.

Art & Cocktails

Karriere

Flæsketorvet 57
+45 33 21 55 09
karrierebar.com
Dybbølsbro
Closed Sun-Wed. Open Thu 8pm-midnight; Fri/Sat 8pm-4am

The brainchild of artist Jeppe Hein and his restaurateur sister Laerke, Kødbyen bar Karriere is at once a creative hub and the go-to spot for understatedly cool Copenhageners in the know. Artists talks and performances are held regularly, vying for creative first place with Karriere's cocktails, the likes of the *Voyeur Baby* and the *Red Cow*. And if you feel like some movement, resident DJs spin beats well into Friday and Saturday nights.

Dedicated to Mixology

Lidkoeb

 Vesterbrogade 72B
+45 33 11 20 10
lidkoeb.dk
København H
Closed Mon. Open Tue-Sat 4pm-2am; Sun 6pm-midnight

Decked out in timber, this pharmaceutical-lab-turned-cocktail bar is Ruby's (p29) Vesterbro cousin. Larger and more laid back, Lidkoeb is equally dedicated to excellence in the mixology department. Sit by the cosy fireplace or, on warmer evenings, outdoors in the 18th century cobbled yard.

Nørrebro

–Multicultural Treasure Trove

Historically Copenhagen's working class neighbourhood, Nørrebro later developed a strong countercultural bent, and is now famous for its multicultural make-up. Tucked away in its cobbled side streets are a plethora of small design shops and high calibre restaurants.

Nørrebro was developed at breakneck speed, at the same time as Vesterbro (p30) and Østerbro (p60), when building outside the city's historical limits was finally permitted in 1853. Its traditional working class population moved to greener pastures in the 20th century, leaving the dilapidated area to those unable to find housing elsewhere. In the 1980s, efforts to redevelop its dense tenements led to violent clashes between the authorities and militant squatters. At the same time, the area's cheap housing attracted immigrants and refugees, many from the Middle East, which in combination with Nørrebro's legacy of high profile crimes, reinforced its image as the "Nørre Bronx".

Today, Nørrebro is visibly Copenhagen's most diverse neighbourhood, especially in its southern fringes along its main street Nørrebrogade, and around Sankt Hans torv, both lined with kebab shops, bars and second-hand boutiques. Nearby Ravnsborggade is famous for its antique shops, which expand their wares onto the pavement in the summer. Further north, the area around picturesque cobbled Jægersborggade is quickly becoming a Copenhagen highlight, dense with speciality design and small fashion shops, proper coffee and top quality cuisine. In the middle of it all lies the historic Assistens Cemetery, the last home of many famous Danes including Søren Kierkegaard, Niels Bohr and H.C. Andersen. A lush green lung in this otherwise dynamic neighbourhood, locals come here to relax.

CARLS
SPECIAL
Carlsberg
Pilsner

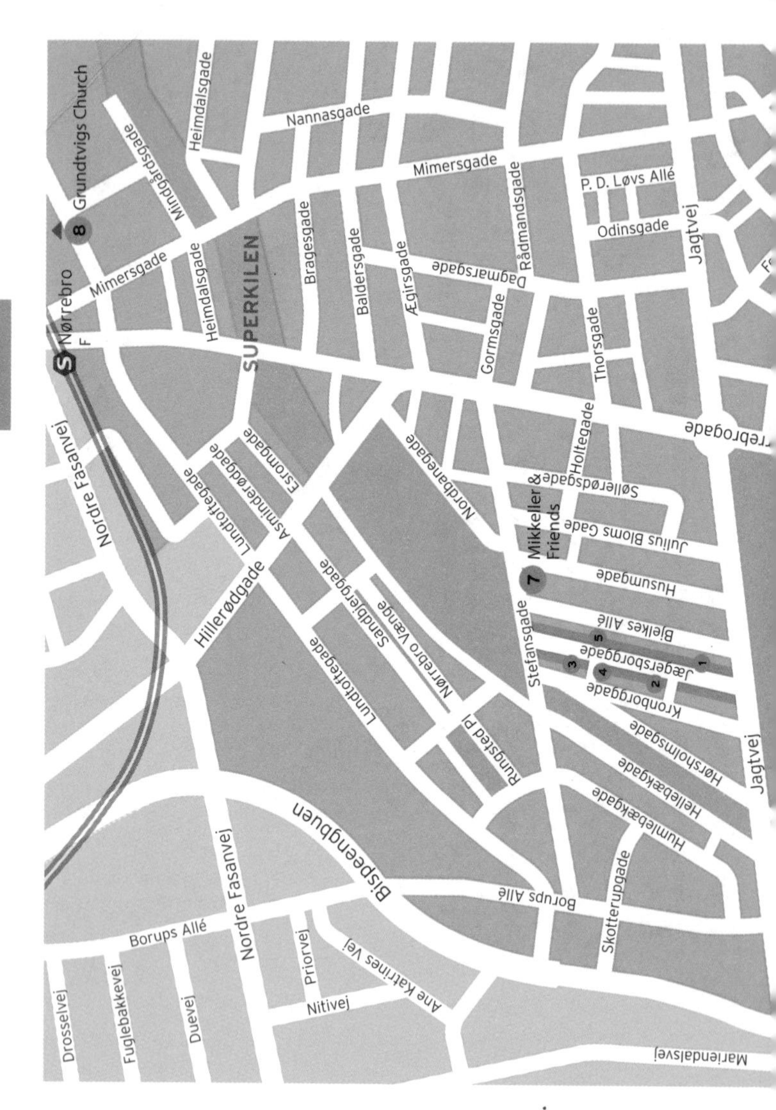

Grundtvigs Church
8
Nørrebro
S
F
Mindegårdsgade
Heimdalsgade
Nannasgade
Mimersgade
Mimersgade
Heimdalsgade
SUPERKILEN
Bragesgade
Baldersgade
Ægirsgade
Dagmarsgade
Rådmandsgade
Gormsgade
P. D. Løvs Allé
Odinsgade
Jagtvej
Thorsgade
Holtegade
Nørrebrogade
Nordre Fasanvej
Esromgade
Asminderødgade
Lundtoftegade
Nordbanegade
Søllerødsgade
Mikkeller & Friends
7
Julius Bloms Gade
Husumgade
Bjelkes Allé
Jægersborggade
Kronborggade
Stefansgade
1
2
3
4
5
Hillerødgade
Sandbjerggade
Nørrebro Vænge
Lundtoftegade
Rungsted Pl
Hørsholmsgade
Hellebækgade
Humlebækgade
Jagtvej
Bispeengbuen
Nordre Fasanvej
Borups Allé
Borups Allé
Skotterupgade
Priorvej
Ane Katrines Vej
Nitivej
Drosselvej
Fuglebakkevej
Duevej
Mariendalsvej

2 Keramiker Inge Vincents
3 Flaco Design
4 Relæ
5 Manfreds & Vin
6 Oysters & Grill
ASSISTENS CEMETERY
NØRREBRO
Sjællandsgade
Meinungsgade
Guldbergsgade
Peter Fabers Gade
Møllegade
Nørre Allé
Birkegade
Elmegade
SANKT HANS TORV
Blegdamsvej
Fælledvej
Sankt Hans Gade
Læssøesgade
Ryesgade
Ravnsborggade
Sortedam Dossering
Nørrebrogade
Baggesensgade
Kapelvej
Griffenfeldsgade
Stengade
Todesgade
Korsgade
Gartnergade
Blågårdscade
Wesselsgade
Smedegade
Ewaldsgade Thorupsgade
Åboulevard
Hans Tavsens Gade
Struenseegade
Rantzausgade
Brohusgade
Ingemannsvej
Svanemosegårdsvej
H. C. Ørsteds Vej
Steenwinkelsvej
Worsaaesvej
J Thomsens Gade
Forum M1/M2
200 metres
FREDERIKSBERG (PAGE 77)
ØSTERBRO (PAGE 62)
INDRY BY (PAGE 10)

Pioneering Roaster

The Coffee Collective

Jægersborggade 10
+45 60 15 15 25
coffeecollective.dk
Open daily. Mon-Fri 7am-7pm; Sat 8am-7pm; Sun 8am-7pm

Copenhagen's distinctive coffee pedigree can be traced back to the opening of The Coffee Collective, the city's first open roastery and coffee shop. The original location on picturesque and now trendy Jægersborggade, Nørrebro's locavore high street, is friendly and unassuming—but the queue lining the cobbled street attests to the potency of its acclaimed brew. Two other locations, one in the buzzy Tovanhalerne Market (p13) and another in an old industrial Fredrikesberg space on leafy Gothåbsvej, are also well worth a visit.

Thinwear

Keramiker Inge Vincents

Jægersborggade 27
+45 40 70 17 50
vincents.dk

Closed Sun. Open Mon/Tue often; Wed/Fri 10am-4pm; Thu 10am-6pm; Sat 11am-3pm

The makers of Jægersborggade go for the lean look. Accordingly, Inge Vincents' elegant contemporary ceramics, called thinwear, give a distinct impression of lightness and movement. Working at the edge of form and function, Vincents molds pieces from high translucency white porcelain clay and creates organic but sophisticated lines, crevices and textures through experimentation in slab technique and wheel throwing. From bowls to vases and tealight vessels, Vincents' designs bring some of the elegance of modernism into the contemporary design scene.

Artisanal Lighting

Flaco Design

Jægersborggade 47
+45 27 21 16 66
flacodesign.dk
Open Sat 11am-7pm and by appointment

In the heart of eco-bobo Jægersborggade, DJ, art, design, and self-confessed lighting junkie Casper Madsen, aka Flaco's workshop/showroom/store is a repository of artfully designed paper-thin handmade raw wood pendants and other lighting items. With designs inspired by nature and sourced and handmade in Denmark, Flaco Design is the place to go for an inspired piece to remind you of the Danish capital once you've returned home.

High Calibre Dining

Relæ

Jægersborggade 41
+45 36 96 66 09

restaurant-relae.dk

Closed Sun-Tue. Open Wed-Sat 5.30pm-midnight; Sat also noon-3pm

Regularly voted one of Copenhagen's best restaurants, Christian F. Puglisi's Relæ melds culinary mastery with unpretentious simplicity. Located on Nørrebro's cultural and culinary hotspot Jægersborggade, across the street from Puglisi's wine bar-cum-restuarant Manfreds (p56), Relæ was founded with the concept of bringing the diner closer to the kitchen and ingredients—the result is high calibre dining in a creative setting. Relæ is top end gastronomy without pretense and cultural associations.

Modern Danish Cuisine & Wine

Manfreds & Vin

 Jægersborggade 40
+45 36 96 65 93
manfreds.dk
Closed Mon. Open Tue-Sun noon-3.30pm, 5.30pm-10pm

Chistian F. Puglisi, formerly of Noma and of current Relæ (p55) pedigree, cooks up an organic/biodynamic storm at this outstanding Nørrebro wine bar/restaurant. Manfreds' stellar collection of hard-to-find cult wines add bite to the dynamic four course menu, where you can sample the best of modern Danish cuisine in a casual and festive atmosphere. And if you're just looking for a good glass of wine, you can drop by the 20-seat bar.

Denmark Meets the Med

Oysters & Grill

6 Sjællandsgade 1B
+45 70 20 61 71
cofoco.dk/oysters
Open daily from 5.30pm

Mallorca meets Alice in Wonderland at this loosely Iberian inspired casual dining spot in a scruffy pocket of Nørrebro. Oysters and Grill brings a collection of surf and turf, from razor clam to flank steak, to the beloved parilla. The brainchild of the Cofoco (Copenhagen Food Company) group, the restaurant's whimsical interior complements its edgy, multicultural Nørrebro surroundings to perfection. So grab a glass of cava and partake in the merriment.

Øl with Flair

Mikkeller & Friends

Stefansgade 35
+45 35 83 10 20
mikkeller.dk
Open daily. Sun-Wed 2pm-midnight; Thu/Fri 2pm-2am; Sat noon-2am

Mikkeller's founder, Mikkel Borg Bjergsø, was a former math and physics teacher with a flair for brewing. In fact, he enjoyed it to such an extent that he enlisted two of his high school students to experiment with different brewing techniques in the school kitchen. The students started a brewery, To Øl, in 2010 and joined forces with their teacher to create Mikkeller, a convivial, well designed modern *bierstube*, complete with turquoise floor, aiming to serve the best renditions of the drink available. And with forty taps and 200 bottles available, you'll be spoilt for choice.

Brick Expressionist Church

Grundtvigs Church

8 På Bjerget 14B
+45 35 81 54 42
grundtvigskirke.dk
Emdrup S
Open Mon-Sat 9am-4pm; Sun noon-4pm (winter until 1pm)

The awe inspiring Grundtvigs Church towers high over the suburbs of northern Copenhagen. The result of a competition held in 1913 to build a church named after the philosopher and national figurehead N. F. S. Grundtvig, it was designed by architect Peder Vilhelm Jensen-Klint. Grundtvigs is a rare example of brick-expressionist church architecture—cleverly combined with Gothic proportions, a minimalist interior and the stepped gables typical of Danish village churches. The church's chairs were designed by Klint's son Kaare, who after his father's death also completed the structure in 1940.

Østerbro & Nordhavn

–Middle Class Copenhagen

A stone's throw from the peaceful Søerne lakes and the large Fælledparken park, Østerbro is Copenhagen's classic middle class neighbourhood of neat tree-lined streets, comfortable cafés and well-stocked interior design shops.

Unlike Vesterbro (p30) and Nørrebro (p48), which were built up quickly to provide cheap housing for the city's 19th century working classes, Østerbro developed slowly as the bourgeoisie built grand villas in a mostly rural setting. The area's growth accelerated at the turn of the century with the opening of the railway from Østerport to the popular resorts along the coast north of Copenhagen (p92). Østerbro became defined by upscale apartment buildings and broad boulevards centred on the busy Trianglen junction and its emblematic "soup terrine" bus shelter building. The extensive docklands and industrial installations of Nordhavn, Copenhagen's vast, new "northern" port, developed just across the rail tracks.

In the mid-20th century, Østerbro's bourgeosie discovered the allures of suburbia and many moved into Copenhagen's wealthy northern suburbs, spanning the beautiful coastline. Still largely residential, Østerbro's magnificent mansions now house embassies and professional practices. Across the tracks, frenzied activity is underway as large swathes of docklands are transformed into a new urban neighbourhood, complete with marinas, cruise ship terminals and, of course, furniture showrooms.

FÆLLEDPARKEN
Tagensvej
Juliane Maries Vej
Frederik V's Vej
Øster Allé
Blegdamsvej
Trepkasgade
Fredensgade
Lundingsg.
Ryesgade
TRIANGLEN
Normann Copenhagen 1
Fru Heiberg 4
Slagelsegade
Østerbrogade
SORTEDAMS SØ
Øster Søgade
Willemoesgade
Classensgade
SØERNE
Øster Farimagsgade
3 Aamanns
Lundsgade
Upsalagade
Stockholmsgade
Dag Hammarskjölds Allé
Sølvgade
National Gallery
Kristianiagade
Trondhjemsgade
Øster Voldgade
Østbanegade
Østerport A/B/C/E/H
Rigensgade
Folke Bernadotte
N
200 metres
NØRREBRO (PAGE 51)
INDRE BY (PAGE 10)
FREDERIKSSTADEN (PAGE 12)

Østerbrogade
G. Adolfs Gade
C. Johans Gade
E. Ohlsens Gade
Rothesgade
Ribegade
Randersgade
Krausesvej
Viborggade
Løgstørfgade
Korsørgade
Vardegade
Århusgade
Silkeborgsgade
Gammel Kalkbrænderi Vej
Strandboulevarden
Hjørringgade
Paustian
2
Nordhavn
A/B/C/E/H
Østbanegade
Marstalsgade
A. F. Kriegers Vej
Petersborgvej
Odensegade
Nordre Frihavnsgade
ØSTERBRO
Lindenovsgade
J Munks Gade
Næstvedgade
Holsteinsgade
Præstøgade
Fiskedamsgade
Livjægergade
NORDHAVN
Kalkbrænderihavnsgade
Arendalsgade
Dampfærgevej

Design Powerhouse

Normann Copenhagen

1 Østerbrogade 70
+45 35 55 44 59
normann-copenhagen.com
Østerport S
Closed Sun. Open Mon-Fri 10am-6pm; Sat 10am-4pm

Normann's flagship store is a Copenhagen design emporium, gathering many of the world's more interesting home design, fashion and accessory brands, alongside its magnificent in-house designs and all the Scandinavian classics. Constantly sourcing the latest trends in interior design, two visits to Normann will never provide the same experience. The shop has won several prizes for innovation in retail and hosts a number of pop-up stores, recently including Tsumori Chisato for Copenhagen Fashion Week.

Waterfront Dining

Paustian

2 Kalkbrænderiløbskaj 2
+45 39 18 55 01
restaurantpaustian.dk
Nordhavn Ⓢ
Open daily. Mon-Sat noon-4pm; Sun 10.30am-3pm

For fresh and innovative Danish cuisine served in a gorgeous waterfront setting, make your way to Paustian. Open only for lunch, Paustian is also a home design warehouse and retail shop, all located in Jørn Utzon's (the architect of the Sydney Opera House) Paustian House. The restaurant space is dominated by clean lines, gorgeous contemporary furniture and stellar views of the yachts in Nordhavn's marina.

Smørrebrød Delight

Aamanns

Øster Farimagsgade 10
+45 35 55 33 44

aamanns.dk

Nørreport M1 M2 S

Etablissement: Closed Mon. Open Tue 11.30am-4pm; Wed-Sat 11.30am-4pm, 6pm-11pm; Sun noon-4pm

Deli: Open daily. Mon-Fri 10.30am-8pm; Sat 11am-4.30pm; Sun noon-4.30pm

Smørrebrød powerhouse by day, Aamann's doubles as an excellent Danish bistro by night. Divided between a more casual Deli and formal restaurant, Aamann's Etablissement, this is the place to sample new takes on the classic Danish open-faced sandwich. Pop by the deli for an easy going lunch, complete with old fashioned herring in ramson, tartare of beef loin with smoked cheese and a smattering of new Danish potatoes with lovage or treat yourself to a full blown meal at Etablissement prepared by chef Magnus Pettersson.

Dramatic Roots

Fru Heiberg

4 Rosenvængets Allé 3
+45 35 38 91 00
fruheiberg.dk
Østerport S
Open daily 5pm-10pm

Cosy, candle lit "Mrs Heiberg" is a Franco-Danish bistro, inspired by the figure of magnetic 19th century actress Johanne Luise Heiberg. As much known as a preserve of the 1800s Copenhagen party scene as a connoisseur of poetry, at once melancholic and spirited, Heiberg embodied the zeitgeist of a Copenhagen in transformation. Today's restaurant, with its intellectually fused menu, artistic ambiance, and tendency towards both the finer and more bohemian aspects of urban life, recaptures the essence of a city in the throes of transformation.

Christianshavn

–Liberal Canal-side Town

Intersected by canals, the formerly independent city of Christianshavn has a distinct maritime and liberal atmosphere. Its charming canals and quaint cobbled streets feel miles away from the bustle of central Copenhagen (p8), just across water.

Christianshavn came into existence in 1618 as part of Danish King Christian IV's ambitious extension of Copenhagen's fortifications. Inspired by the thriving city of Amsterdam, the swampy terrain between the capital and the island of Amager was drained by canals and filled with merchants' warehouses. After only 35 years, the small merchant and garrison town was swallowed up by rapidly expanding Copenhagen, but has retained a unique, laid-back feel to this day. Historically working class, the area's picturesque canals developed a bohemian vibe in the 1970s. Its liberal tendencies are famously accentuated in the "Freetown Christiania", a hippie commune on the site of an abandoned military barracks. Partially self-governing, the authorities long tolerated the residents' open-minded attitudes about narcotics, though recent efforts have been made to normalise affairs in the *staden* ("the town").

Today, Christianshavn is a quiet and popular residential area just steps from the frenzy of the capital's centre. The neighbourhood's core around Christianshavns Torv is dotted with friendly canal-side cafés and bars. In the north, Holmen's former warehouses and military installations are home to creative businesses, new housing developments and the city's 2004 opera, one of the most modern—and expensive—in the world. To the south, the former B&W shipyard is now the site of modern corporate offices.

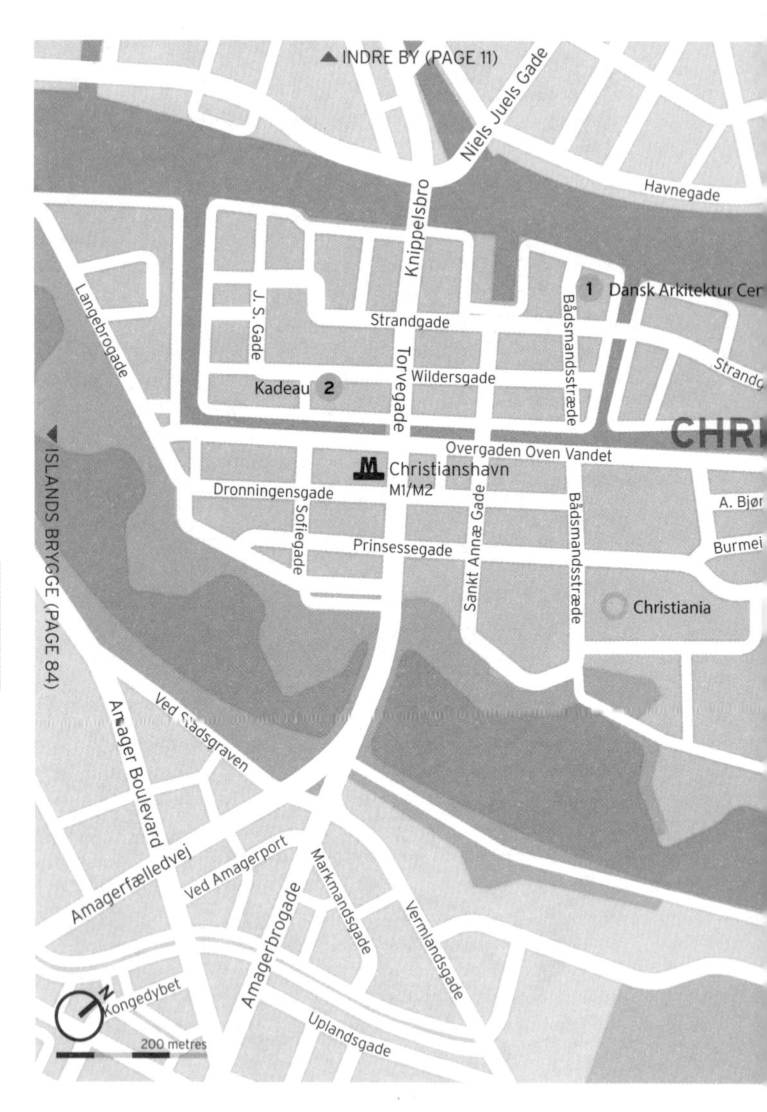
INDRE BY (PAGE 11)
Niels Juels Gade
Havnegade
Knippelsbro
Langebrogade
J. S. Gade
1
Dansk Arkitektur Cer
Strandgade
Bådsmandsstræde
Strandg
Torvegade
Wildersgade
Kadeau
2
CHR
ISLANDS BRYGGE (PAGE 84)
Overgaden Oven Vandet
Christianshavn
M1/M2
Dronningensgade
Sofiegade
Sankt Annæ Gade
Bådsmandsstræde
A. Bjør
Burmei
Prinsessegade
Christiania
Ved Stadsgraven
Amager Boulevard
Amagerfælledvej
Ved Amagerport
Markmandsgade
Amagerbrogade
Vermlandsgade
Kongedybet
N
200 metres
Uplandsgade

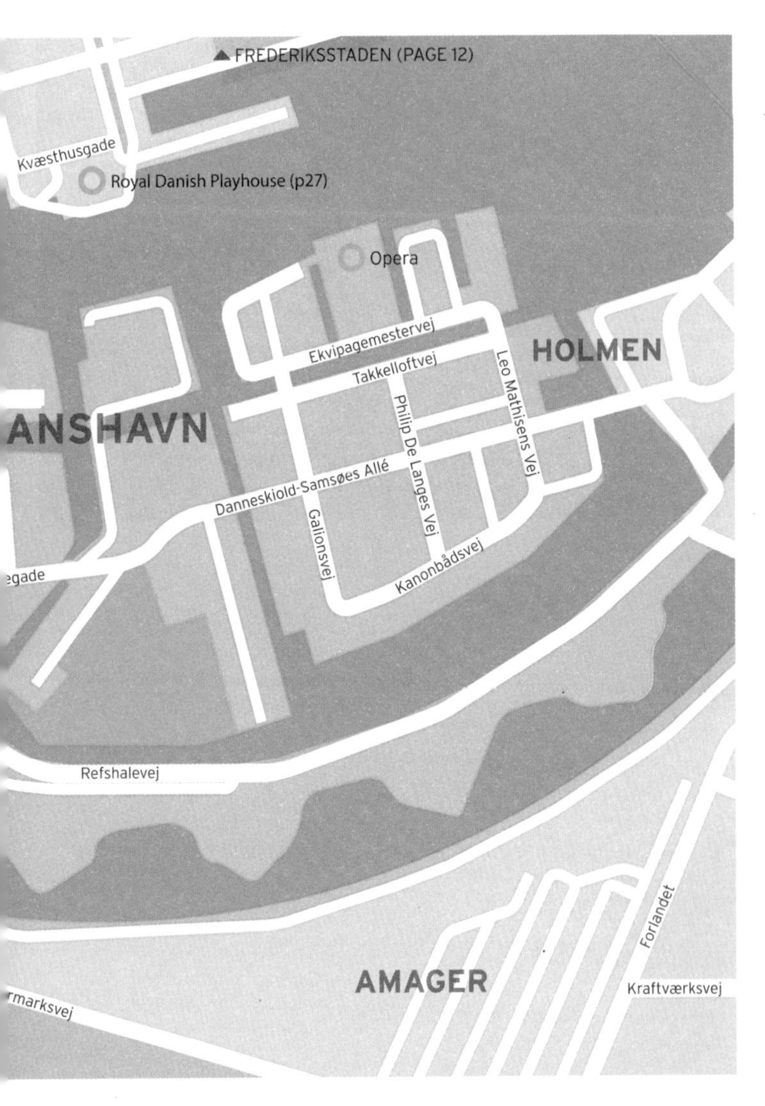
▲ FREDERIKSSTADEN (PAGE 12)
Kvæsthusgade
Royal Danish Playhouse (p27)
Opera
Ekvipagemestervej
Takkelloftvej
HOLMEN
Leo Mathisens Vej
Philip De Langes Vej
ANSHAVN
Danneskiold-Samsøes Allé
Galionsvej
Kanonbådsvej
egade
Refshalevej
Forlandet
AMAGER
Kraftværksvej
rmarksvej

Quayside Architecture

Dansk Arkitektur Center

1 Strandgade 27B
+45 32 57 19 30
dac.dk
Christianshavn M1 M2

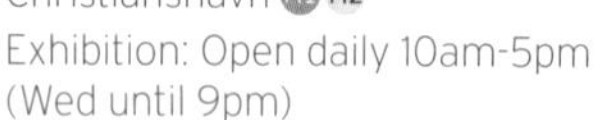

Exhibition: Open daily 10am-5pm (Wed until 9pm)
Café: Open daily. Mon-Fri 11am-4pm (Wed until 8pm); Sat/Sun 10am-4pm
Admission DKK 40 (€5.50)

The Danish Architecture Centre was created in 1985 to develop and communicate knowledge of architecture, urban planning and sustainable development. The DAC's quayside headquarters in a 19th-century former warehouse, has a comprehensive bookshop, regularly hosts exhibitions, and functions as a social centre for Copenhagen's architecture and design scene. The upper level café boasts some of the best views over Copenhagen's harbour.

A Taste of Borholm

Kadeau

Wildersgade 10A,
+45 33 25 22 23

kadeau.dk

Christianshavn M1 M2

Closed Sun/Mon. Open Tue-Sat from 6pm

Located on a picturesque cobbled street at the heart of Christianshavn, Kadeau brings a Michelin-starred taste of the conifer-laced Baltic island of Borholm to the city. One of the pioneers of the New Nordic movement, the restaurant has won many accolades—its sous-chef Morten Falk was recently given the first prize at the Danish Chef of the Year awards. With its weathered wood and herb-laden, laid-back look, this is certainly one of the most enjoyable spots to sample exquisite experimental Nordic cuisine.

Frederiksberg

–Bourgeois Inner-city Suburb

Surrounded by Copenhagen on all sides and home to many of its elites, Frederiksberg is actually an independent city and only de facto part of the Danish capital. As Copenhagen's traditional entertainment district, similar to Berlin's interwar "New West", Frederiksberg still boasts numerous theatres and cinemas, though it is now more famous for its refined residents and leafy villa districts.

Frederiksberg dates back to 1651 when King Frederik III founded a village west of Copenhagen and gave twenty Dutch peasants the right to farm along Allégade. Farming, however, was not successful and the land eventually reverted to the Crown. The area's fortunes turned in 1699 when King Frederik IV decided to build a palace—the "Danish Versailles"—on a nearby hill, which was duly renamed "Frederiksberg". Proximity to the King's court made its houses coveted by Copenhagen's elites, who turned them into country houses. In the summer months, restaurants catered to the flow of visitors from the capital. When building restrictions were lifted in 1852, Frederiksberg saw a rush of development on its western edge along the road to Copenhagen. As a wealthy holiday town increasingly intertwined with the capital, Frederiksberg became the city's upmarket entertainment district, boasting cinemas, theatres, cafés, bars and Copenhagen's zoo.

Frederiksberg's privileged heritage is still visible in its generous parks, wide boulevards, lavish villas, and, of course, the Baroque Frederiksberg Palace, now an officer's academy. Mostly residential, its high streets are lined with gourmet delis, galleries and numerous theatres. Frederiksberg's highlight is certainly Værnedamsvej, located at the border with trendy Vesterbro (p30). The street is known locally as "food street" for its concentration of speciality food stores and high calibre restaurants.

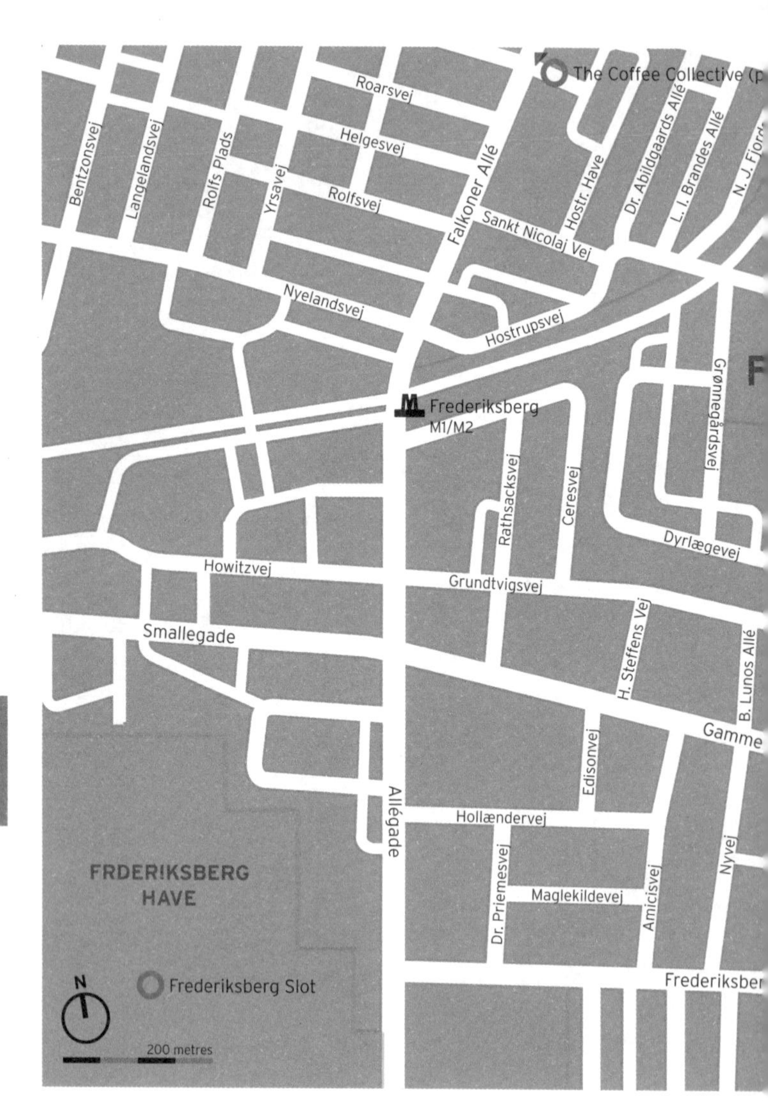
The Coffee Collective (p
Roarsvej
Helgesvej
Rolfsvej
Bentzonsvej
Langelandsvej
Rolfs Plads
Yrsavej
Falkoner Allé
Sankt Nicolaj Vej
Hostr. Have
Dr. Abildgaards Allé
L. I. Brandes Allé
N. J. Fjord
Nyelandsvej
Hostrupsvej
Frederiksberg
M1/M2
Grønnegårdsvej
Rathsacksvej
Ceresvej
Dyrlægevej
Howitzvej
Grundtvigsvej
Smallegade
H. Steffens Vej
B. Lunos Allé
Gamme
Edisonvej
Allégade
Hollændervej
Dr. Priemesvej
Maglekildevej
Amicisvej
Nyvej
FRDERIKSBERG HAVE
N
Frederiksberg Slot
200 metres
Frederiksber

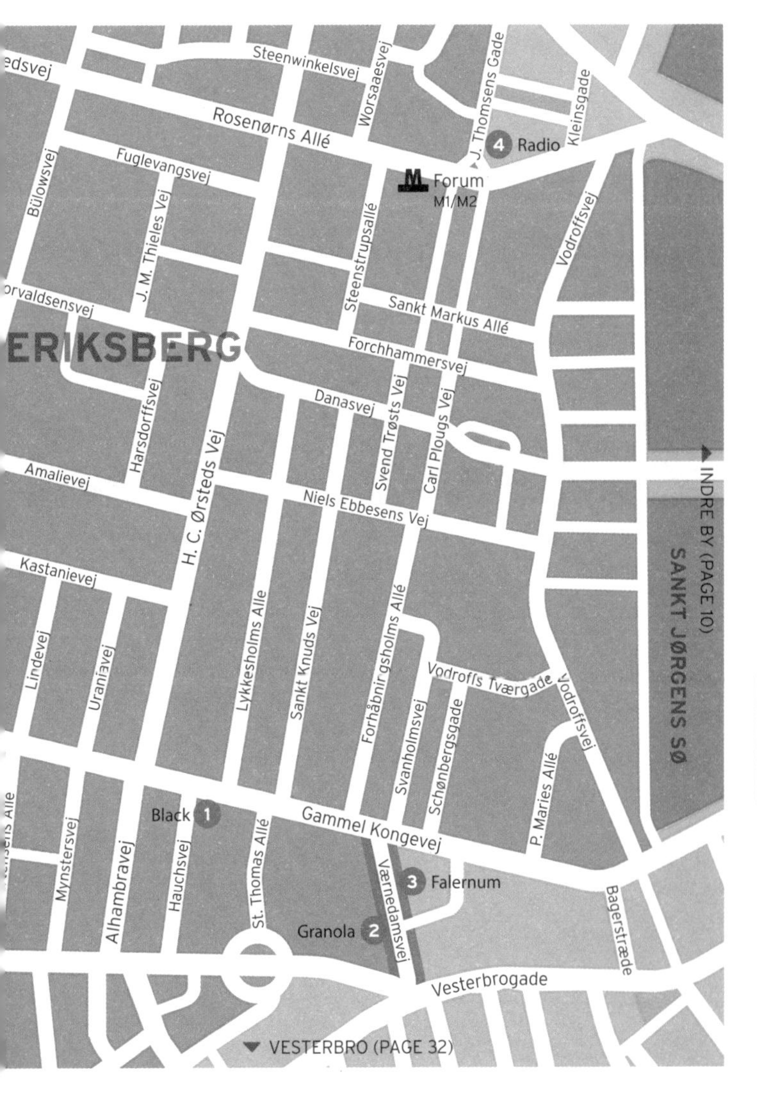

Steenwinkelsvej
Worsaaesvej
J. Thomsens Gade
Kleinsgade
Rosenørns Allé
4 Radio
Fuglevangsvej
Bülowsvej
Forum
M1/M2
J. M. Thieles Vej
Steenstrupsallé
Vodroffsvej
Sankt Markus Allé
ERIKSBERG
Forchhammersvej
Danasvej
Harsdorffsvej
Svend Trøsts Vej
Carl Plougs Vej
Amalievej
H. C. Ørsteds Vej
Niels Ebbesens Vej
INDRE BY (PAGE 10)
SANKT JØRGENS SØ
Kastanievej
Lindevej
Lykkesholms Allé
Sankt Knuds Vej
Forhåbningsholms Allé
Vodroffs Tværgade
Svanholmsvej
Schønbergsgade
P. Maries Allé
Black 1
Gammel Kongevej
Mynstersvej
Alhambravej
Hauchsvej
St. Thomas Allé
Værnedamsvej
3 Falernum
Granola 2
Bagerstræde
Vesterbrogade
VESTERBRO (PAGE 32)

Visual Inspiration

Black

1 Gl Kongevej 103
+45 35 10 73 27
anneblack.dk
København H S
Closed Sun. Open Mon-Fri 11am-6pm; Sat 10am-3pm

Danish ceramicist Anne Black's concept store features Black's own intricate contemporary porcelain collection. The airy shop also displays other highlights of Danish textile and home design. Decorated with freshly cut wild flowers and the latest in design literature, a visit to Black provides a refreshing dose of visual inspiration.

The Brunch Place

Granola

Værnedamsvej 5
+45 40 82 41 20

København H

Open daily. Mon-Fri 7am-midnight; Sat 9am-midnight; Sun 9am-4pm

A neighborhood institution, Granola is the place to go for an invigorating brunch or an afternoon cup of coffee with the daily paper. Wildly popular, the attractive and sunny café attracts patrons from every walk of life, from bobos to hipsters to mothers. And the food is scrumptious too.

Vino-centric Frederiksberg

Falernum

Værnedamsvej 16
+45 33 22 30 89
falernum.dk
København H
Open daily. Mon-Fri noon-midnight; Sat/Sun noon-2am

Owned by the same vino-centric Husted brothers as Bibendum (p28), Falernum is another top-notch wine bar on buzzing Værnedamsvej. Wine friendly dishes predominate at this establishment and the atmosphere could not be more convivial. Decked out in thick wooden slabs, the bar's walls are adorned with rows of bottles sourced by Husted wines, the owners' wine import company, and can all be purchased for home consumption.

Local Pizzazz

Radio

Julius Thomsens Gade 12
+45 25 10 27 33
restaurantradio.dk
Forum M1 M2
Closed Sun-Mon. Open Tue-Thu 5.30-midnight; Fri/Sat noon-3pm; 5.30pm-midnight

Living by the motto "the kitchen of Radio follows the seasons day by day", Radio supplies a daily list of up to the minute forageable ingredients that will make it into the restaurant's delightful palette of dishes. Neighbouring the city's old radio house from which it takes its name, the restaurant is warm, urbane and sophisticated—but strongly connected to its local environment. Sourcing produce from its own Copenhagen plot, local fishermen, farmers and orchards, Radio provides a winning combination of astonishingly good cuisine, locally driven fare, and urban pizzazz.

Islands Brygge

–Harbourfront Copenhagen

Amager, the island opposite Copenhagen's city centre, and Islands Brygge, its embankment, are at once contemporary Copenhagen's famous waterfront of well designed public harbour baths and apartment buildings and, further inland, a rather traditional Copenhagen neighbourhood. The area's highlight, especially in the summer, is *Havneparken* ("Harbour Park"), a 2-kilometre stretch of redeveloped walkway along the city's harbour.

Today's Islands Brygge was underwater until the late 19th century when it was reclaimed for military facilities—the area's main street is still called Artellerivej ("Artillery Way"). From 1901 the port authorities created new areas for bulk storage to the south. Islands Brygge (literally "Iceland Quay") became the hub for the lucrative trade with Iceland, then a Danish dependency, which contributed to the wealth of 18th century Copenhagen under Frederick IV. By the mid-20th century the area's military installations and docklands had fallen out of use, leaving behind a post-industrial wasteland at the heart of the city. In 1983, the northern area near the Langebro bridge was transformed into a park, which was subsequently extended southward, accompanied more recently by large scale contemporary housing developments.

Further inland, Amager was historically Copenhagen's quiet working class backwater, literally located at a dead end at the edge of the country. Everything changed with the advent of the Øresund Bridge, which placed Amager at the heart of the new cross-border metro region. In its wake came the development of Ørestad, a large scale, slightly soulless, new neighbourhood, complete with metro line, and state of the art facilities for Denmark's national broadcasting service and Copenhagen's university.

▲ CHRISTIANSHAVN (PAGE 70)
1 CPH Living
Langebrogade
Vester Voldgade
ulevard
Langebro
Amager Boulevard
Ørestads Boulevard
4 Harbour Bath
Puggaardsgade
HAVNEPARKEN
Thorshavnsgade
Klaksvigsgade
Hambrosgade
▲ VESTERBRO (PAGE 33)
Mitchellsgade
Njalsgade
Egilsgade
Gunløgsgade
Bergthorasgade
Isafjordgade
Leifsgade
Halfdansgade
ISLANDS BRYGGE
Islands Brygge
Snorresgade
Sturlasgade
Artillerivej
Kalvebod Brygge

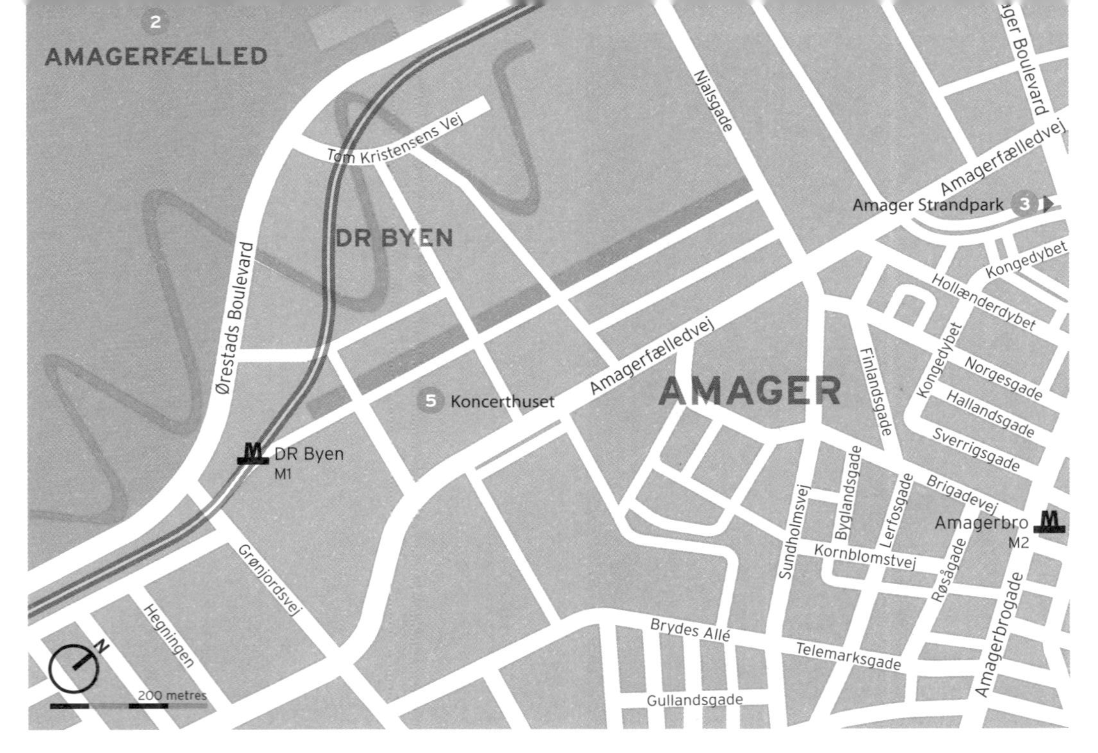
AMAGERFÆLLED
2
ager Boulevard
Amagerfælledvej
Amager Strandpark
3
Kongedybet
Hollænderdybet
Norgesgade
Hallandsgade
Sverrigsgade
Brigadevej
Amagerbro
M2
Amagerbrogade
Røsågade
Lerfosgade
Kornblomstvej
Finlandsgade
Byglandsgade
Sundholmsvej
Telemarksgade
AMAGER
Njalsgade
Amagerfælledvej
Brydes Allé
Gullandsgade
Koncerthuset
5
DR BYEN
Tom Kristensens Vej
DR Byen
M1
Ørestads Boulevard
Grønjordsvej
Hegningen
200 metres
N

Boating Nights

CPH Living

Langebrogade 1
+45 61 60 85 46
cphliving.com
Christianshavn M1 M2
Doubles from DKK 1,180 (€158)/night incl. tax

Two elements seem to define contemporary Copenhagen: design and water. Located on a boat moored in centrally located but ruggedly "left bank" Islands Brygge, CPH takes the latter as its starting point and offers onboard accommodation with stunning city and waterfront views. The houseboat boutique hotel offers all the modern conveniences, supplemented by maritime steel and wood inspired Danish design pieces in a unique and romantic setting.

Natural Exercise Grounds

Amagerfælled

2 Ørestads Boulevard
DR Byen M1
Public access

The Amagerfælled common is a vast nature reserve extending far into the centre of Copenhagen on the island of Amager. Historically a grazing area that was occassionally flooded, under Christian IV, the Amagerfælled was turned into a training ground and shooting range for the nearby barracks at Islands Brygge. Until 1845, it was also used for executions. A conservation area today, the Amagerfælled is widely enjoyed by joggers, sunbathers, school groups and bird watchers.

Beach and Seaside Park

Amagar Strandpark

3 Øresundsstien 11
+45 26 30 24 82
amager-strand.dk
Øresund M2
Public access

The expansive 5 km stretch of beach on the eastern coast of Amager island provides a less crowded alternative to Klampenborg's Bellevue Strand (p92) and the city's harbour baths (p89) in the summer months—or a vast deserted idyll for a winter dip. The beach and the wooden Helgoland bathing facility date back to the 1930s but saw a major revamp in 2005, when the sandy artificial island and lagoon and state-of-the- art facilities were added.

A Dip in the City

Islands Brygge Harbour Bath

4 Islands Brygge 7
+45 23 71 31 89

Islands Brygge M1, København H S
Open daily (June-August). Mon-Fri 7am-7pm; Sat/Sun 11am-7pm
Admission DKK 35 (€4.70)

Oddly yet unsurprisingly it is in Copenhagen, a chilly Scandinavian city, that a busy commercial port and a thriving harbour bathing scene have come to co-exist. Followed by an extensive cleanup of the city's harbour and sewers, the first bath opened at Islands Brygge for the 2002 swimming season. The current 2003 facility has a total of five pools for swimming, diving and children, and caters to Copenhageners from all walks of life, from families to workers from the nearby offices. Plans to extend the bathing season with a winter bath are in the making.

Flamboyant Concert Hall

Koncerthuset

5 Emil Holms Kanal 20
+45 35 20 62 62
dr.dk/koncerthuset
DR Byen M1
Regular performances. Refer to website for program

Part of the larger DR Byen (Danish Radio Town) development complex, the Koncerthuset is the most expensive concert hall in the world to date. Jean Nouvel's sculptural piece of contemporary architecture is also Denmark's premier concert house, hosting the Danish National Symphony and Chamber Orchestras and visiting jazz, classical, choral, rock and pop performers from across the world.

Northern Suburbs

–Posh Seaside Resorts

Set amidst a landscape of parks, lakes, and golf courses, Copenhagen's northern suburbs, locally known as the whiskybæltet ("whiskey belt"), are notoriously wealthy. The 40-kilometre Øresund shore, reaching all the way to Hamlet's Kronborg castle at Elsinore, is dotted with attractive Victorian seaside resorts boasting both high-calibre museums and beautiful beaches.

The countryside north of Copenhagen, with its vast forests, has long had noble connections and is dotted with palaces, including the Danish royal family's spring and autumn residence at Fredensborg, fourty kilometres north of the city. In the 19th century, the resorts on the Øresund coast and its glamorous main artery Strandvejen, became a favourite weekend destination for Copenhageners escaping the industrialising city. Klampenborg, located at the foot of the Jægersborg Dyrehave, the royal hunting ground, drew particularly large crowds to its Dyrehavsbakken amusement park and nearby horse racing tracks, both still in operation today. Klampenborg is also were designer Arne Jacobsen had his first major commissions, which came to define Danish modern design. These include Bellevue Beach (p99) and the famous 1936 Skovshoved petrol station. The advent of the automobile opened the countryside to the middle classes, and by the 1970s the area's wealthy resort towns and old villages had become enmeshed with large swathes of suburbia.

Today, the seaside resorts along the Øresund shore continue to attract large numbers of visitors from Copenhagen and beyond. Aside from royal mansions, beaches and a beautiful landscape, the towns have also made a name for themselves thanks to numerous highbrow museums and galleries, including the world-famous Louisiana Museum of Modern Art (p96).

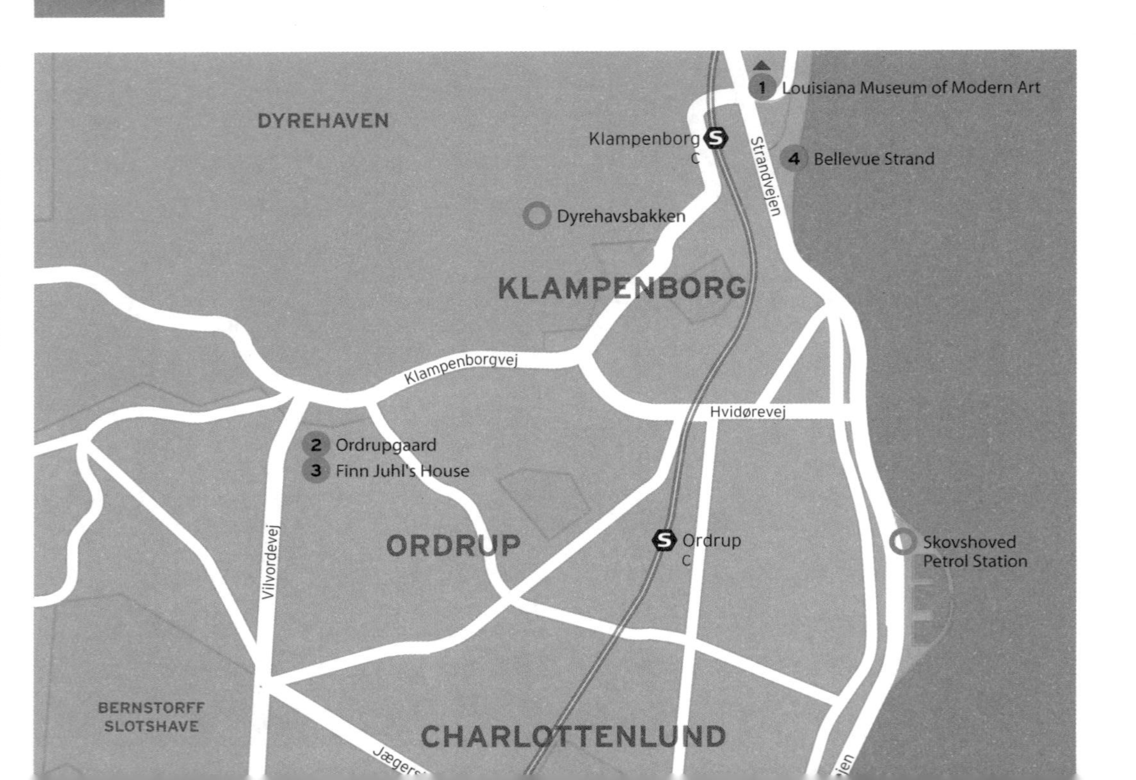
1 Louisiana Museum of Modern Art
DYREHAVEN
Klampenborg
Strandvejen
4 Bellevue Strand
Dyrehavsbakken
KLAMPENBORG
Klampenborgvej
Hvidørevej
2 Ordrupgaard
3 Finn Juhl's House
Vilvordevej
ORDRUP
Ordrup
Skovshoved Petrol Station
BERNSTORFF SLOTSHAVE
CHARLOTTENLUND

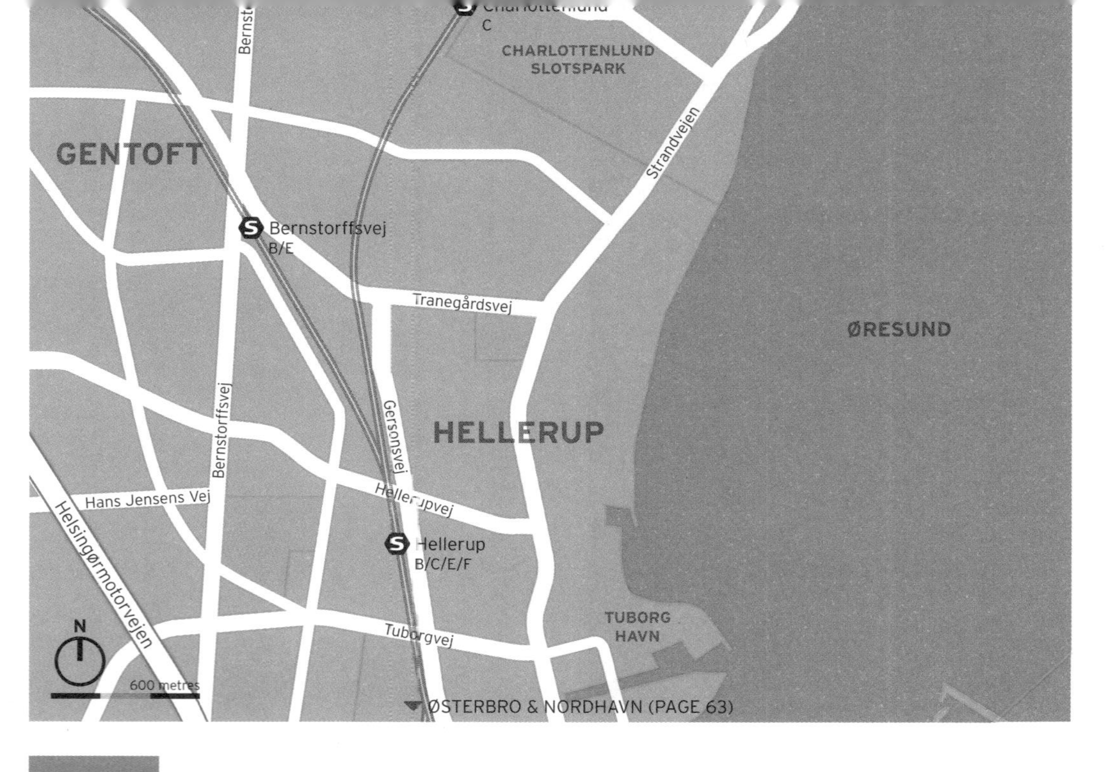
CHARLOTTENLUND SLOTSPARK
GENTOFT
Strandvejen
Bernstorffsvej B/E
Tranegårdsvej
ØRESUND
Gersonsvej
HELLERUP
Bernstorffsvej
Hans Jensens Vej
Hellerupvej
Hellerup B/C/E/F
Helsingørmotorvejen
TUBORG HAVN
Tuborgvej
N
600 metres
ØSTERBRO & NORDHAVN (PAGE 63)

Art on the Sound

Louisiana Museum of Modern Art

Gl Strandvej 13, Humlebæk
+45 49 19 07 19

louisiana.dk

Öresundståg train service to Humlebaek

Closed Mon. Open Tue-Fri 11am-10pm; Sat/Sun 11am-6pm

Admission DKK 110 (€14.50)

Perhaps the most magical spot in the Greater Copenhagen area, the Louisiana Museum of Modern Art ranks amongst the world's premier modern art galleries (the Asger Jorn gallery is a highlight) and is also an architectural gem set amidst the stunning backdrop of the Øresund sound. A summer visit would not be complete without a visit to the restaurant, with its Danish buffet, mid-century furniture, and views over the Henry Moore sculptures and wild flowers spilling onto the pebbly beach beneath.

Art Amid the Dears

Ordrupgaard

2 Vilvordevej 110, Charlottenlund
+45 39 64 11 83

ordrupgaard.dk

Klampenborg Ⓢ, then bus 388 to Vilvordevej

Closed Mon. Open Tue-Fri 1pm-5pm (Wed until 9pm); Sat/Sun 11am-5pm

Admission DKK 110 (€14.50)

Located in Copenhagen's urban forest, the Jægersborg Deer Park, Odrupgaard is a modern art museum focusing on French impressionism as well as masterpieces from the Danish Golden Age. The romantic setting is complemented by Zaha Hadid's black lava concrete-cast New Wing and its ultra-fluid design. Every summer Odrupgaard sponsors an "Art Park" featuring site-specific concepts by renowned contemporary artists. Round up your visit with a *smørrebrød* and coffee at the musem's café.

Design Icon

Finn Juhl's House

Vilvordevej 110, Charlottenlund
+45 39 64 11 83

ordrupgaard.dk

Klampenborg Ⓢ, then bus 388 to Vilvordevej

Closed Mon-Fri. Open Sat/Sun 11am-4.45pm

Admission DKK 110 (€14.50), part of Ordrupgaard museum (p97)

Pathbreaking designer and architect Finn Juhl is perhaps best known for his "Danish Modern" furniture design. His 1940s pieces redefined Danish design, and work he undertook on the interior design of the UN's "Trusteeship Chamber" in New York was considered a breakthrough. Items such as Finn Juhl's iconic tray are now omnipresent in Copenhagen's design boutiques and still feel remarkably fresh. Now part of Ordrupgaard (p97), Finn Juhl's House offers great insight into the designer's life, work (he designed the house himself) and sources of inspiration.

Arne Jacobsen's Beach

Bellevue Strand

4 Strandvejen 340, Klampenborg
+45 39 90 06 95
bellevuestrandbad.dk
Klampenborg S
Public access

Klampenborg's 700 metre Bellevue Beach is at once Copenhagen's most popular beach and a Danish design classic. Opened in 1932, the beach and the surrounding area were one of the first commissions of Arne Jacobsen, whose modern design concept included everything from lifeguard towers to kiosks and changing rooms. Just around the corner are the Jacobsen-designed Bellevue Theatre and Bellavista apartment complex, and not far behind the beach begins the tranquil Dyrehaven woodland.

Essentials

Airport Transfer

Located just 8 kilometres south of the city on the island of Amager, Copenhagen's Kastrup Airport (CPH) is the second busiest airport in Scandinavia and Scandinavian Airlines' main hub. Taxis are usually available at Arrivals at Terminals 1 and 3. The ride into central Copenhagen takes about 20 mins, depending on traffic, and costs around DKK 250-300 (€33-40).

Terminal 3 is located directly on the mainline railway connecting Copenhagen with Malmö across the Øresund bridge, making the train a quick option into central Copenhagen and beyond. The Øresund trains run every 10 mins during the day and 1-3 times per hour at night. The ride to Copenhagen's Central Station takes about 15 mins. The airport is also connected to the centre by line M2 of the Copenhagen Metro. Trains run every 4-6 minutes during the day and evening and around every 15-20 minutes at night. The ride to Nørreport in central Copenhagen takes around 15 mins. Standard Copenhagen public transport tickets (see below) are valid on the Metro and all trains into Copenhagen.

Taxis

Taxis are not as commonly used in Copenhagen as in, say, New York, but they are usually available at main stations and booking them over the phone or online is hassle-free and reliable. Fares are not cheap and a 15-minute trip across the inner city can easily amount to DKK 200 (€27) or more. The largest taxi company is Taxa 4x35 (+45 35 35 35 35, taxa.dk). It is worth mentioning that though not a systematic problem, drivers of less reputable taxi companies occasionally attempt to overcharge for rides.

Public Transport

Opened in 2002, Copenhagen's fully automatic Metro is one of the most modern and comfortable in Europe. There are two lines, both of which run from the Amager island through the city centre into Frederiksberg. Trains run 24 hours a day in 2-4 minute intervals during rush hours and up to every 20 minutes on weekdays after midnight. A large expansion to the Metro, the "City Ring", is scheduled to open in 2018, connecting all of Copenhagen's inner-city neighbourhoods. The Metro is complemented by commuter S-Trains, connecting Copenhagen's suburbs with a trunk line running through the city centre. The S-Trains operate from 5am to 12.30am and run every 5-10 minutes.

Public transport fares are based on a sophisticated system of zone rings—however, given that all of central Copenhagen is located in zone rings 1 and 2 and the minimum ticket always covers 2 zone rings, the simple rule is that a single ticket for travel in central Copenhagen costs DKK 24 (€3.20). The airport is located in the third (yellow) zone ring from the centre, meaning that a single ticket covering 3 zone rings is required, at a cost of DKK 36 (€4.80). The same arithmetic applies to the entire Copenhagen region, so that a ride from the centre to, say, Klampenborg in zone ring 4 requires a ticket covering 4 zone rings, at DKK 4 x 12 = 48 (€6.40). A City Pass for unlimited travel in central Copenhagen and to/from the airport is available for 24 hrs for DKK 75 (€10) or 72 hrs for DKK 190 (€25.50). The classic paper-based 10-ride knippekort will be phased out in 2014. All tickets are valid for interchange with metro, bus, trains and harbour buses.

Tipping

Similar to elsewhere in Europe, Denmark does not have an elaborate tipping tradition; service is normally included in restaurants, hotels and taxis and staff are usually well paid. That said, tips are of course appreciated for exceptionally good service, in which case 5-10% is commonly given.

Safety

Copenhagen is a very safe, prosperous Scandinavian city, and as such, once common big city precautions have been taken, one should be extremely unlucky to fall victim to crime—parents famously leave their babies unattended in prams outside shops and restaurants. One thing to note is that petty thieves are known to operate around the busy areas near the Central Station and the Tivoli amusement park.

Index

S

T

V

W

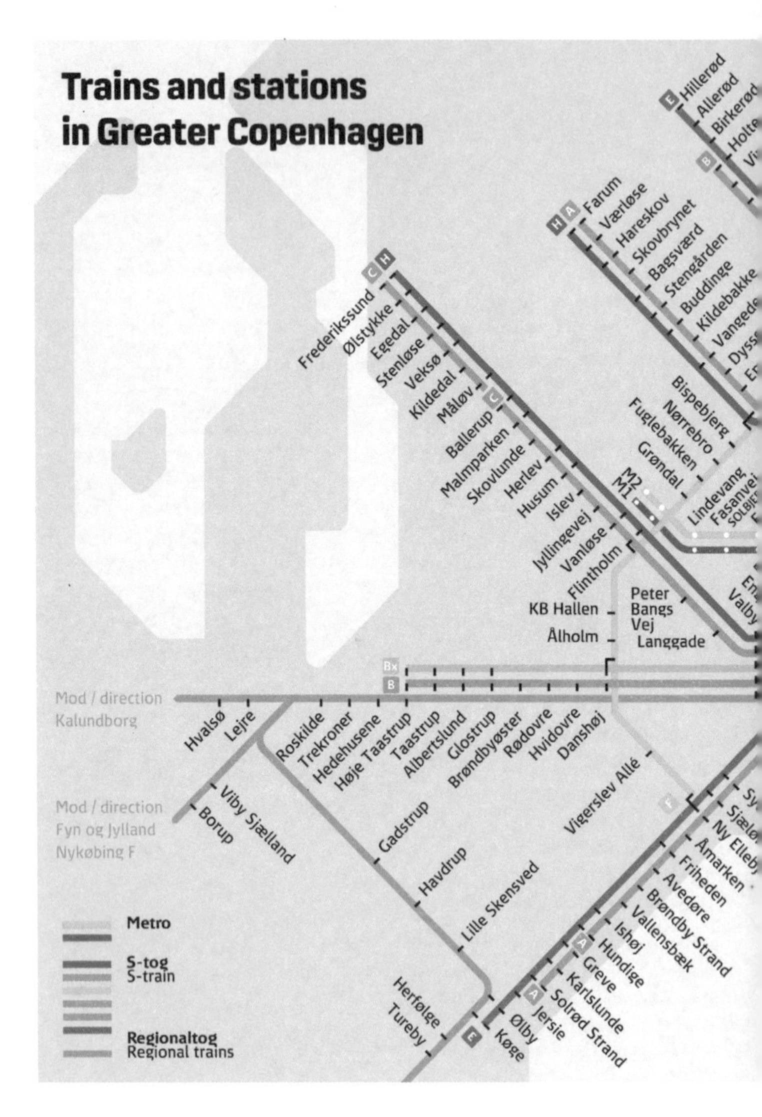
Trains and stations in Greater Copenhagen
Hillerød
Allerød
Farum
Værløse
Hareskov
Skovbrynet
Bagsværd
Stengården
Buddinge
Kildebakke
Frederikssund
Ølstykke
Egedal
Stenløse
Veksø
Kildedal
Måløv
Ballerup
Malmparken
Skovlunde
Herlev
Husum
Islev
Jyllingevej
Vanløse
Flintholm
Bispebjerg
Nørrebro
Fuglebakken
Grøndal
M2
M1
Lindevang
KB Hallen
Ålholm
Peter Bangs Vej
Langgade
Valby
Bx
B
Mod / direction Kalundborg
Hvalsø
Lejre
Roskilde
Trekroner
Hedehusene
Høje Taastrup
Taastrup
Albertslund
Glostrup
Brøndbyøster
Rødovre
Hvidovre
Danshøj
Vigerslev Allé
Mod / direction Fyn og Jylland Nykøbing F
Viby Sjælland
Borup
Gadstrup
Havdrup
Lille Skensved
Herfølge
Tureby
Køge
Ølby
Jersie
Solrød Strand
Karlslunde
Greve
Hundige
Ishøj
Vallensbæk
Brøndby Strand
Avedøre
Friheden
Åmarken
Metro
S-tog
S-train
Regionaltog
Regional trains

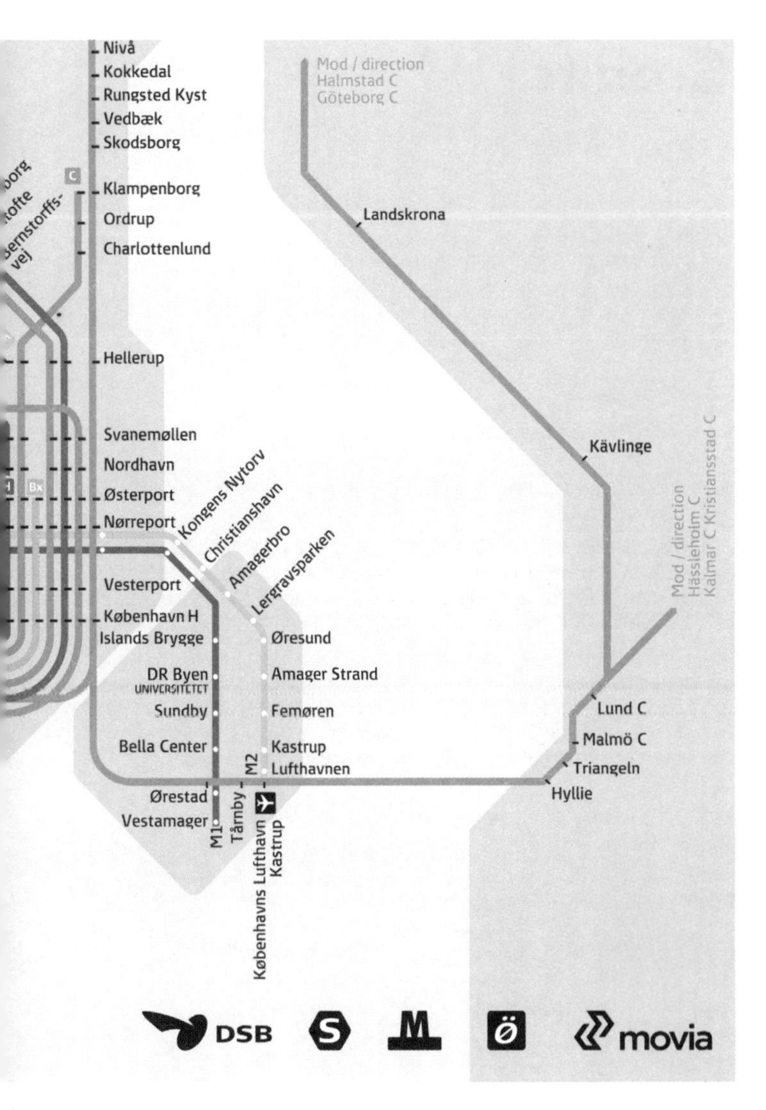
Nivå
Kokkedal
Rungsted Kyst
Vedbæk
Skodsborg
Klampenborg
Ordrup
Charlottenlund
Hellerup
Svanemøllen
Nordhavn
Østerport
Nørreport
Vesterport
København H
Kongens Nytorv
Christianshavn
Amagerbro
Lergravsparken
Islands Brygge
DR Byen
Sundby
Bella Center
Ørestad
Vestamager
M1
Tårnby
Øresund
Amager Strand
Femøren
Kastrup
Lufthavnen
M2
Københavns Lufthavn Kastrup
Mod / direction
Halmstad C
Göteborg C
Landskrona
Kävlinge
Mod / direction
Hässleholm C
Kalmar C Kristianstad C
Lund C
Malmö C
Triangeln
Hyllie
DSB
movia

Credits

Published by Analogue Media, LLC
244 5th Avenue, Suite 2446, New York, NY 10001, United States

Edited by Alana Stone
Layout & Production by Stefan Horn

For more information about the Analogue Guides series, or to find out about availability and purchase information, please visit analogueguides.com

First Edition 2014
ISBN: 978-0-9838585-8-4

Typefaces: Neutraface 2, Myriad Pro and Interstate
Paper: Munken Lynx

Printed in Barcelona by Agpograf, S.A.

Analogue Media would like to thank all contributing venues, designers, manufacturers, agencies and photographers for their kind permission to reproduce their work in this book.

Cover design by Dustin Wallace
Proofread by John Leisure
Metro Map by Jørn Damsgaard, Damsgaard & Lange MAA MDD

All photography credited to the listed venues unless stated otherwise:

Indre By (9/13/14/16) Stefan Horn (17) Anders Hviid for Dinesen (18) Karsten Bundgaard (19) Stefan Horn (21) Anders Bergh (22/23/24) Stefan Horn (25) Line Lorentzen (26) Stefan Horn (27) Peter Funch (28) Miklos Szabo Photography (29) Stefan Horn

Vesterbro (31) Stefan Horn (34) Jon Nordstrøm (35) Tom Solo (36/37) Stefan Horn (38) Egon Gade (39) Stefan Horn (40) Thomas Ibsen (41) Stefan Horn (42) Miklos Szabo Photography (43) Marie Louise Munkegaard (44) Line Lorentzen (45) Stefan Horn

Nørrebro (49) Stefan Horn (52) Maria P (53) SOLK Fotografi (54) Stefan Horn (55) © Per-Anders Jörgensen / ALONGSIDE IMAGE (57) Line Lorentzen (59) Maciej Lulko

Østerbro & Nordhavn (61) Stefan Horn (66) Columbus Leth (67) Stefan Horn

Christianshavn (69) Stefan Horn (72) Hanne Hvattum (73) Marie Louise Munkegaard

Frederiksberg (75/78/79) Stefan Horn (80) Miklos Szabo Photography (81) Anders Schønnemann

Islands Brygge (83) Stefan Horn (87) Adrian Lazar (88) Photo: Jens Bladt, www.planfoto.dk (89) Eva Fabricius (90) Bjarne Bergius Hermansen

Northern Suburbs (93) Stefan Horn (96) Lars Ranek/Louisiana (97) Tobias Toyberg (98) Anders Sune Berg (99) Diana Lee

About the Series

–A Modern Take on Simple Elegance

Analogue Guides is a series of curated city guidebooks featuring unique, high quality, low key venues—distilled through the lens of the neighbourhood.

Each neighbourhood is complemented by a concise set of listings, including restaurants, cafés, bars, hotels and serendipitous finds, all illustrated with photographs. The listings are supplemented by custom designed, user-friendly maps to facilitate navigation of the cityscape. Venues featured in the guides score high on a number of factors, including locally sourced food, tasteful design, a sophisticated and relaxed atmosphere and independent ownership.

Analogue Guides are designed to complement the internet during pre-travel preparation and smartphones for on-the-ground research. Premium photography and a select choice of venues provide an ideal starting point for pre-travel inspiration. At your destination, the guides serve as portable manuals with detailed neighbourhood maps and clear directions.

The result: a compact, efficient, effervescent manual celebrating the ingenuity of the contemporary metropolis.